· THE COMPLETE ·

INDIAN

INSTANT POT®

COOKBOOK

THE COMPLETE
INDIAN
INSTANT POT®
COOKBOOK

130 TRADITIONAL & MODERN RECIPES

AUTHORIZED BY INSTANT POT®

CHANDRA RAM

Photographs by Huge Galdones

Robert
ROSE

The Complete Indian Instant Pot® Cookbook
Text copyright © 2018 Chandra Ram
Photographs copyright © 2018 Galdones Photography
Cover and text design copyright © 2018 Robert Rose Inc.

Instant Pot and associated logos are owned by Double Insight Inc. Used under license.

Library and Archives Canada Cataloguing in Publication

Ram, Chandra, 1972–, author
The complete Indian Instant Pot cookbook : 130 traditional
& modern recipes / Ram Chandra.

Includes index.
"Authorized By Instant Pot".
ISBN 978-0-7788-0611-0 (softcover)

1. Cooking, India. 2. Pressure cooking. 3. Cookbooks.
I. Title. II. Title: Indian Instant Pot cookbook.
TX724.5.I4C43 2018   641.5954   C2018-903791-1

Disclaimer
The recipes in this book have been carefully tested by our kitchen and our tasters.
To the best of our knowledge, they are safe and nutritious for ordinary use and users. For those
people with food or other allergies, or who have special food requirements or health issues,
please read the suggested contents of each recipe carefully and determine whether or not they
may create a problem for you. All recipes are used at the risk of the consumer.

We cannot be responsible for any hazards, loss or damage that may
occur as a result of any recipe use.

For those with special needs, allergies, requirements or health problems, in the event of any
doubt, please contact your medical adviser prior to the use of any recipe.

Cover and book design: Laura Palese
Cover and interior photography: Galdones Photography
Editor: Meredith Dees
Copyeditor, Proofreader and Indexer: Gillian Watts
Recipe Editor: Jennifer MacKenzie
Food and Prop Styling: Christina Zerkis and Chandra Ram

Published by Robert Rose Inc.
120 Eglinton Avenue East, Suite 800, Toronto, Ontario, Canada M4P 1E2
Tel: (416) 322-6552 Fax: (416) 322-6936
www.robertrose.ca

Printed and bound in Canada

1 2 3 4 5 6 7 8 9 TCP 26 25 24 23 22 21 20 19 18

TO MY PARENTS, who met,
fell in love, married, moved to America,
raised children across three
cultures, cooked and lived and taught me
how to navigate the mishmash
of food and life.

CONTENTS

INTRODUCTION

IT WAS THE SAME FEELING EVERY TIME. My parents, brothers and I would depart the airplane, struggling under our piles of carry-on luggage overflowing with Mad Libs, decks of airline playing cards, books and magazines packed to entertain two adults and four children for 22 hours of travel (or as I like to call it, the Kentucky–Charlotte–New York–Germany–Delhi–Vizag route to Grandma's house). Bone-tired but wide awake after drinking sweet, milky tea from Hamburg to New Delhi, we'd push through customs and immigration, then exit the dim glare of the airport arrivals lounge into the night air. I'd inhale, breathing in that weirdly captivating blend of cleaning solution, gasoline and toasted cardamom, and smile as my uncles swept me up in a giant hug. Even as a child I knew that India was mine, and that I was hers in some way. I may never have felt totally at home in India, but it has always felt like part of me.

We were "the Americans"—my Indian father, Irish mother and three brothers—part of the family but different from everyone else. We'd visit every other year, landing in Delhi and then taking trains to Vizag, my father's small hometown where my grandparents still lived, to meet the aunts, uncles and cousins who would join us there for a few weeks from their homes in Delhi, Kanpur, Hyderabad and Calcutta.

Once in Vizag, we'd settle into our visit. A dozen hours off from our usual time zone, my brothers and I would spend our first few days still drowsy with jet lag, and our nights playing hour after hour of cards when sleep wouldn't come (if three solid hours of playing War doesn't do the trick, you aren't ever going to get to sleep). People might stare at us while we walked to the candy store or went to the beach in that small town, but ambling along amid a gaggle of uncles, aunties, and cousins, we belonged. We may have not spoken any of the languages or understood what to do in the Hindu temples, but we were still part of the clan, if a little different.

In some ways it wasn't so different when we were home in Kentucky, where a stranger might approach me at the grocery store to ask where I came from, and no one could pronounce my name. I wasn't white enough to fit in with the other kids at school, but not Indian enough to run with the crowd at the Indo-American Civic Society. Like my parents, I said things like "the phone line is engaged," much to my friends' amusement, and turned beet red when my mother packed the Indian dessert called *barfi* in my lunch (I was in the third grade!). At home, we had an "Indian cabinet" in our kitchen that reeked of pungent, funky asafoetida and cumin—one I prayed that my friends would avoid when we foraged for cookies during sleepovers. India sometimes felt uncomfortable, but it wasn't always easy to be in America, either.

The Indian Americans I know feel the same way. America is our home, but some part of us identifies as Indian—we're not completely one or the other. We don't want to let go of Indian culture as our parents were encouraged to do when they immigrated a generation ago, but we don't always know how to claim it for ourselves.

Although I was interested in food and cooking, even there it was hard to find footing. At home in Kentucky, I spent hours in the kitchen with my mother, an adventurous cook who made everything from the scones she'd grown up eating in County Wexford to South Indian dosas, Japanese stir-fries and giant gingerbread houses. But in India the kitchen was off-limits; my grandparents' cook held court, and curious young American visitors weren't welcome.

And—to be honest—I didn't always love the food. At the long dining table in my grandparents' house, my cousins downed tangy idlis doused with spicy sambar for breakfast while my brothers and I ate instant oatmeal and peanut-butter-and-jelly sandwiches, needing a break from the unfamiliar. When we ate curried vegetables, my (lame!) American palate couldn't handle the heat, so my aunties would patiently spoon demerara sugar and yogurt onto my food to tame it. My love of coconut proved to be the gateway to several dishes; spoon a little coconut chutney on top of anything and I'd try it.

FROM LEFT TO RIGHT: With my grandparents before a big party at their house in Vizag; rocking a serious ponytail game on the beach at the Bay of Bengal; my grandfather helping me with garlands from the market; helping sort rice in the courtyard of my grandparents' house.

But even as I grew up and went on to study in culinary school, cook in restaurants and then embark on a career in food writing, I didn't have as strong a background in Indian food as I would have liked. I knew how to throw a few dishes together, but felt as if I was just replicating the greatest hits from my childhood, not exploring the cuisine. I understood only snippets of that vast culture people shove into a single box and label "Indian."

So when people tell me they are too intimidated to cook Indian food, I get it. There are the unfamiliar spice blends; the need to remember to soak your lentils, chickpeas and rice; and the time it takes to braise meats into fork-tender bites, not to mention the fear of using a "will it blow up?" stovetop pressure cooker.

Weirdly, it took buying a modern piece of cooking equipment to bring generations of family meals back into my kitchen. Once I had the epiphany of making butter chicken in 20 minutes instead of an hour, I knew I had found the key to making Indian cooking manageable. The Instant Pot® opened a door to making me feel connected to my family and our food traditions, even while living a whiplash-fast American life. I could cook chana masala on a weeknight (starting with dried chickpeas!); make rasam at the first sign of a cold; and look my visiting auntie in the eye and tell her that I was making—not buying—my lime pickle.

This book was created to make cooking Indian food as unintimidating as any other cuisine. It incorporates my Indian heritage, my upbringing in the American South, and the years I spent learning French cooking techniques in culinary schools and expanding on that cooking in restaurants. Are these recipes truly "authentic"? Well, they are authentic to me, to being a "third-culture" kid, to my experiences as an Indian Irish American. You'll find both traditional and modern recipes within these pages, recipes from all over India, or inspired by Indian cooking, that meld Indian ingredients and American sensibilities to create dishes for novices and experts alike. And it's all made easier by the Instant Pot®. **—CHANDRA**

BASICS

WHY INDIAN FOOD IS
PERFECT FOR THE INSTANT POT®
(AND VICE VERSA)

A pressure cooker is key to cooking Indian food. It transforms rock-hard lentils and rice into smooth stews and curries, and braises meat in a fraction of the time it would take otherwise. Stovetop pressure cookers can be found on propane stoves in kitchens all over India. They allow you to cook even if the power goes out, which is important for people in both large cities and the rural parts of the country. Indian expats who grew up using stovetop pressure cookers continue to use them regularly in America, but the fact that you have to watch over them (or risk an explosion) means they aren't very convenient. Many people have tried to adapt their family recipes for slow cookers, which are more accessible here, but that takes an investment of time and planning that is hard to maintain.

So when a friend told me about the Instant Pot, I was curious. I'm not a gadget person (and I don't have room for them in my apartment kitchen), but I was intrigued by the convenience factor. An electric pressure cooker means you can explore—and pull off—traditional recipes without worrying over a stovetop pressure cooker. Unlike with most slow cookers, you can sauté vegetables and brown meat in the same pot you'll use to braise them, saving the need to use multiple appliances and dishes.

The Instant Pot replaces a pressure cooker, slow cooker, rice cooker, yogurt maker, bread proofer and steamer. Even better, it seems to do the impossible by giving us room in our lives to breathe. Suddenly, time-consuming cooking projects like making yogurt, leavening bread dough and braising meats and vegetables are doable on a weeknight, without taking hours or having to babysit your dinner as it cooks. It is a lifesaver for anyone, but for Indian Americans and anyone interested in cooking Indian food, it's a game-changer that makes both traditional and modern Indian cooking fast and easy. Dried lentils and chickpeas cook in minutes, even when they haven't soaked for hours (or even days). Rice is perfectly cooked in as little as three minutes. Homemade yogurt can be made to the particular tanginess and texture of a not-forgotten grandmother's standards. And it's all hands off—you don't have to babysit the Instant Pot like a stovetop pressure cooker or listen for it to whistle so you know your food is cooked.

All that functionality of the Instant Pot made Indian cooking accessible to me, and I hope it will do the same for you too.

A FEW INSTANT POT TIPS
TO KEEP IN MIND

GETTING STARTED

This might sound incredibly basic, but there are two things about your Instant Pot that you should check every time you start cooking. First, make sure the sealing ring is in place; you don't want to find out that it isn't when your machine is unable to pressurize. If it's not secure, you'll see steam escaping from the sides once you start cooking. If that happens, simply turn off the machine, release any pressure that has built up, and remove the lid. Press the sealing ring in place and start over again, subtracting a couple of minutes from your cooking time. No harm, no foul.

Second, it's so easy to forget to turn the pressure valve to Sealing, which you need to do unless you are steaming a cake or using the Yogurt or Slow Cooker function. You'll notice if it's not in the right position, because steam will release from it and it will hiss at you. Try to remember to always check it when securing the lid.

Many recipes in this book start with the Sauté function, which allows you to brown your ingredients. This is an important step for developing flavor and toasting your spices, so don't skip it. Once the Instant Pot heats up, the Sauté portion of cooking can go fast, so make sure you have all your vegetables and aromatics chopped or ground and ready to cook. After using the Sauté function, you can switch right to pressure cooking. The machine builds up pressure by sealing in air as it raises the temperature, so you need to account for that amount of time in the cooking process (I've included it in the total time amounts listed for each recipe, along with cooking time and the amount of time needed to release the pressure). The amount of food and liquid you have in the inner pot will impact how long it takes to build pressure. You can speed that up by not filling the inner pot more than halfway and by heating the liquid in the recipe before adding it to the pot. But in general, plan on at least 10 minutes to build pressure.

RELEASING PRESSURE

You can release pressure naturally (by letting the machine sit until the temperature inside drops enough for the pressure to diminish) or by quick-releasing it (by toggling the steam valve to the Venting position). As a general rule, let the pressure release naturally for at least a few minutes when cooking meat; doing so allows the meat to rest for a few minutes, like when you let it rest after grilling or roasting it. Natural pressure release is also best when cooking porridge or grains (so any foam in the pot doesn't shoot out the pressure valve) and when cooking rice; the final minutes are important for getting the light, fluffy texture you want. I use the quick-release method when cooking tender vegetables and seafood, to stop the cooking immediately so they don't overcook. For many of the recipes in this book, you'll let the pressure release naturally for a few minutes before quick-releasing the remaining pressure. When quick-releasing the pressure, be sure to use a spoon or spatula to turn the pressure valve, and keep your face away from the vent so you don't burn yourself in the steam as it's released.

SLOW COOKER CONVERSIONS

You can easily convert slow cooker recipes to an electric pressure cooker if you want to speed things up. It takes a little trial and error, but as a basic guideline, slow cooker recipes that call for 4 to 8 hours of cooking can be pressure-cooked in 8 to 30 minutes, depending on the meat used (poultry usually takes 8 to 10 minutes; beef and lamb take more like 20 to 30 minutes). Start by using the Poultry and Meat buttons for dishes that feature those proteins. After the pressure is released, check to make sure the meat's cooked through and adjust from there; you can always add a few minutes after cooking or simmer your dish using the Sauté function.

STOVETOP PRESSURE COOKER CONVERSIONS

To convert stovetop pressure cooker recipes to the Instant Pot, add a little more liquid to the pot than the recipe calls for—I usually add about ½ cup (125 mL) more—and cut the cooking time by a few minutes. If you are working from a recipe that measures the cooking time by number of whistles, time how long it takes to reach those whistles in your stovetop pressure cooker and then take a few minutes off when cooking in the Instant Pot. Then congratulate yourself that you'll never have to listen for those damn whistles again!

COOKING FROM FROZEN

You can also use the Instant Pot to cook or thaw food from frozen, with much better results than you get from a microwave. Just pour ¾ to 1 cup (175 to 250 mL) water or broth into the inner pot and add the frozen food. If you are cooking or thawing frozen meat, soup or stew, secure the lid and cook on high pressure for about 12 minutes to start; frozen vegetables will cook much faster, in as little as a minute for peas or asparagus. When it's done, quick-release the pressure, remove the lid and check the food. If it isn't fully thawed, either pressure-cook it again for a few minutes or simmer it, using the Sauté function on Normal with the lid off, until it's done. If you have a frozen cooked meal in an ovenproof dish, you can reheat it using the Steam function: place the container on the trivet that comes with most Instant Pot models and steam for 15 to 20 minutes to heat it up. It's easy, tastes better and it yields a much better texture than the microwave.

TOOLS

There are a few extra tools used in this book that you might want to consider picking up:

CANNING JARS: I like to store my pickles and chutneys in canning jars. They are easy to sterilize and useful for reheating leftovers in the Instant Pot.

CHEESECLOTH: You'll need this for straining yogurt or paneer. It's available in most grocery stores and hardware stores.

COFFEE/SPICE GRINDER: I grind my spices in an old coffee grinder I've repurposed just for spices (see page 20 for more information).

FOOD PROCESSOR: I use my regular food processor to purée sauces and vegetable dips. I also have a mini food processor that I use regularly to mince small amounts of garlic and ginger; it's a small investment that has paid off by saving time for me over and over again (I really hate mincing ginger by hand).

BLENDER (PREFERABLY HIGH-POWERED): Several recipes call for blending soups or cashews soaked in milk. You can get away with using a regular blender for most of the dishes, but you'll have a hard time blending cashews for kormas in anything other than a high-powered blender.

IDLI STEAMER: If you are interested in making idli, pick up an idli steamer from any Indian grocery or housewares store, or online. Make sure you buy one that is 6 inches (15 cm) in diameter, so it will fit in the standard Instant Pot.

IMMERSION BLENDER: An immersion blender will help you quickly purée a soup in the inner pot without having to transfer it to the blender.

INSTANT POT TRIVET: Most Instant Pots come with a metal trivet you can use for steaming everything from broccoli to cakes, but if you don't have one, it's an inexpensive and worthwhile purchase. I use mine when fermenting dough and batters with the Yogurt function, as well as when steaming food.

METAL BAKING PAN WITH REMOVABLE BOTTOM: I use a 7-inch (18 cm) diameter baking pan has a separate flat base that you can push up through the top of the pan to remove cakes after cooking. You'll need it for making cakes and bread in the Instant Pot. If you can't find one, a 6-inch (15 cm) springform pan will also work; just make sure it fits into the inner pot even with the latch on the side. You can also bake/steam cakes using insert pans sold for use in stovetop pressure cookers. Simply fold a 12-inch (30 cm) piece of aluminum foil into thirds and place it in the pan before adding the crust or cake batter, to create a sling. After the cake cools, loosen it from the edges of the pan with a knife and then use this sling to remove the cake from the pan.

SOUFFLÉ DISH (6- to 7-inch/15 to 18 cm diameter) OR RAMEKINS (4 oz/125 mL): You'll use these to steam cakes and puddings, but they can also be used to help with meal prep and serve sauces.

STAND MIXER OR HANDHELD ELECTRIC MIXER: I'd love to be more old-school about this, but frankly I much prefer having some electric power behind me when beating cake batters and eggs. It adds the air needed to make a cake that is light, not tough.

HOW TO BUILD AN INDIAN MEAL

When I'm putting together an Indian meal, I like to think about balance. If you combine samosas, a creamy meat curry, a giant bowl of biryani, a plate piled high with naan and a hefty scoop of rice pudding, you're going to hate yourself later. Remember—balance, friends. If you're craving a bowl of Butter Chicken (page 206), don't pair it with another rich and creamy stew like Navratan Korma (page 150). Instead, serve it alongside a light vegetable dish like Matar with Feta (page 140) and a little plain rice dressed with raita (pages 56 to 62), or Naan (page 252), but not necessarily both. Save the biryani for a main course, not a side. That being said, create a meal that suits your tastes, regardless of whatever rules you've read somewhere (or that I'm listing right now). On the next page are a just a few helpful guidelines that I've learned over the years to help you craft an Indian meal.

- **KEEP A FEW SWEET AND SAVORY CHUTNEYS AND PICKLES IN THE REFRIGERATOR,** so you'll always have some options on hand. They can be lifesavers when you need to throw a meal together; a little lime pickle, for example, turns a bowl of leftover vegetables and rice into dinner. There are tons of options available at the supermarket, or you can make them from this book (pages 78 to 95).

- **FOR A WEEKNIGHT MEAL,** stick to making a single dal, meat or vegetable curry and serve it with rice or bread, raita and chutney or pickle. You can cut any of the savory dishes in half to make fewer portions or double them to make more (as long as you don't overfill the inner pot). Don't try to reduce or double the dessert recipes, though; if I can live with extra cake in my freezer, so can you.

- **FOR A DINNER PARTY,** I always make a couple of snacks, because I am a huge believer in the snacking cocktail hour—maybe Potato Pea Samosas (page 100) and a chutney, plus something unexpected, like Fried Chili Paneer (page 113). For my version of a less intense dinner party, I'd make a dip like Spiced Carrot Bharta (page 99) and serve it with crackers and cut-up vegetables, following it with a one-pot meal like biryani, then a dessert that can be made in advance, such as cheesecake. It's just as impressive, and a little easier on you as the host. Or, depending on the crowd that night, I make a meat curry, a vegetable, a dal, rice, naan or roti, raita, chutney and a dessert. It's a lot, but my friends know I'm a little crazy, and at least no one leaves my place hungry.

- When you are trying to make all of the above in a single Instant Pot, **PACE YOURSELF** (trust me on this one; I've been there). Chutneys and pickles can be made a week or more in advance. Meat curries, lentils, desserts, samosa fillings, yogurt, dips and steamed cakes can be made the day before you intend to serve them; the extra time to sit helps the flavors develop. I usually proof bread dough early in the day so that I can free up my Instant Pot to cook vegetables in the late afternoon. I save the rice to cook at the last minute so it's fresh, light and fluffy.

WHAT TO DRINK WITH INDIAN FOOD

The first rule of beverage pairing is to drink what you enjoy, and this is particularly true of India, which doesn't have a long tradition of wine and food.

Beer and Indian food make a classic pairing; the carbonation in beer tends to clean and refresh your palate in between bites of food. When it comes to beer, you might think from its name that an IPA (India pale ale) is the best call for Indian food, but the beer actually got its name because it was shipped to India and developed its strong, hoppy, bitter flavor during the months on board the boat. Bitterness tends to magnify spicy-hot flavors, which is why I prefer to drink lagers that don't compete with the flavors in the food. I also like malty Belgian-style beers; the subtle sweetness of the malt is a nice complement to the spices.

With wine, I will follow the classic pairing of Riesling with Indian food, but since I don't enjoy wines that are sweet, I prefer a dry Riesling from Germany or the Alsace region of France. Pinot Blanc and Gewürztraminer are other good choices. Fruit-forward red wines such as Rioja and Beaujolais also play nicely with Indian food, as do Cabernet Francs and Syrahs.

THE INDIAN PANTRY

So, about those spices . . .

For some reason, people are (unnecessarily, I swear) intimidated by the spices in Indian food. Do me a favor and go into this with an open mind. Indian food is nothing without the spices that cooks grind, toast and combine with unmatched talent. But that doesn't mean all Indian food is spicy-hot. A lot of the dishes in this book don't have any heat but have loads of flavor . . . from spices.

Where to start? First, if you can't remember when you bought your spices, go out and buy some new ones. Same if you remember when you bought them and it was more than a year ago. If you're not sure, sniff your spices. Do they smell like jars of dusty nothing? Go and buy new ones. I'm serious. It's a small expense that is completely worth it. Why go through all the trouble of cooking if half of your ingredients are old/rancid/muted by age? You want your spices to smell like . . . spices.

When you flip through these pages, you'll probably find a few spices that you already own, such as cumin, fennel, cinnamon, cloves and turmeric. Pick up some mustard seeds, coriander seeds and green cardamom pods at the store, and you'll be able to make a lot of the recipes in this book. Pretty easy, right?

GRINDING SPICES

Which brings me to my next point. When in doubt, buy whole spices and, if you don't already have one, a spice grinder (a repurposed coffee grinder works well). Whole spices retain their flavor much better than ground. If you grind as you cook, or at least grind smaller amounts than what you can buy, you will almost always have fresh-ground spices on hand for food emergencies. I use a coffee grinder I bought 20 years ago that I later retired and now use just for spices (so my coffee doesn't smell like cumin). When I need ground coriander or fenugreek, I throw a few coriander or fenugreek seeds in there and voila—it's fast and easy. Just remember to let the spices settle before you remove the lid of your grinder, lest you find yourself amid a cloud of just-ground dried chiles (don't ask me how I learned this). Run a spoonful of uncooked rice through your grinder in between spices to clean it.

TOASTING SPICES

Next, you need to know how to toast your spices. When an Indian tastes your food and comments that the spices are a little raw, that's throwing some serious shade—don't let it happen to you. Spices are toasted to bring out their flavors and to dry them out so they will grind better, even after sitting in a warm tropical environment. There are three different ways to toast spices: dry-roasting in a skillet, tempering in oil to be poured over the finished dish, or frying them with onions cooking in oil (*bhunoo*ing). With each method you start with the whole spices, then add the ground spices toward the end of cooking, so they don't burn in the time it takes to toast the whole spices.

To dry-roast on the stove, simply place the spices in a dry skillet over medium heat. Toast them, shaking the pan frequently so they don't burn, for about 1 minute if ground or 2 minutes if whole, until they are fragrant. To temper spices, heat a few tablespoons of vegetable oil in a skillet over medium heat (or in the inner pot, using the Sauté function on Normal) for 1 minute, then add the spices and cook for 1 to 2 minutes, until they are fragrant.

To *bhunoo* spices, add them to a sautéed chopped onion. Cook for least 1 minute or up to 3 minutes, stirring, until fragrant. In the name of saving time and not using multiple pans, I usually cook my spices with the onion for most dishes. Whatever method you choose, toast your spices slowly, especially the ground spices. Burnt spices taste burnt, not robust.

SPICE LIST

Here are some of the spices you'll use when cooking through these recipes. You can find everything in this book in Indian/Asian or general grocery stores or online.

AJWAIN SEEDS boast an anise flavor, similar to that of oregano or thyme.

AMCHUR POWDER gets its tart flavor from the dried green mangoes used to make it. It adds a tart-sweet flavor without using the liquid from citrus juices.

ASAFOETIDA is also called *hing*. I call it the MSG of Indian cooking because it's got a deeply funky smell when you take a whiff from the jar but adds an underlying boost of flavor to your food. It's added to a lot of lentil dishes to aid in digestion.

CARDAMOM, both green and black, is available in pods, seeds and ground. Green cardamom is floral and herbaceous, while black cardamom is more intense. Use the whole pods when cooking rice dishes, the seeds or ground for infusing a sauce, and ground when mixing into a sauce or dessert.

CORIANDER is floral and pairs nicely with green vegetables. You can buy the round seeds and use them whole or grind them as needed.

CUMIN is also called *jeera* and is available in seeds and ground. I usually buy seeds and grind them as needed. Its slightly bitter, toasty flavor is unparalleled; I go through tons of cumin.

FENUGREEK is also known as *methi* and is available as leaves and seeds (which are dried and ground). It lends a gentle bitterness to food, balancing other flavors.

MUSTARD SEEDS come in brown/black and yellow, and both add a nutty flavor to dishes when heated in oil and popped. Brown or black mustard seeds are more pungent, while yellow mustard seeds are milder.

NIGELLA SEEDS are also known as onion seeds and boast a mild onion flavor. Their jet-black appearance is distinctive, so they are often sprinkled atop bread.

KASHMIRI CHILI POWDER looks like cayenne, so you might think it's spicier than it really is. It's actually one of the gentler spice powders out there, although heat levels vary from brand to brand and crop to crop. If you can't find Kashmiri chili powder, blend 3 parts sweet paprika with 1 part cayenne pepper.

TURMERIC is ginger's golden cousin and is available fresh and dried. I usually use ground dried turmeric. Turmeric is used both in cooking and to dye clothes, which is a gentle reminder that, yes, turmeric will stain your clothes (and your hands and your cutting board).

MAKE YOUR OWN MASALAS
(SPICE BLENDS)

Masala means "mix." I want to give you a few quick recipes so you can make your own spice masalas and won't feel you have to buy something just to make a recipe from the book. The masala recipes that follow make enough to use in a recipe and have a little left over. You don't have to limit their use to Indian food. Sprinkle them over popcorn; toss them with roasted potatoes or fries; use them to season roasted veggies, roast or fried chicken or scrambled eggs or give your avocado toast or hummus a burst of flavor. These will keep for up to two months when stored in a cool, dry place.

CURRY POWDER

*This is the most recognizable Indian spice blend, known for its bright
yellow color and often used to season and color chicken curries. There are as many
versions of curry powder as there are homes in India, but this fairly mild one is a good
starting point. Add more Kashmiri chili powder if you'd like it to be hotter.*

MAKES ¼ CUP (60 ML)

Coffee/spice grinder

4 teaspoons (20 mL) **coriander seeds**
2 teaspoons (10 mL) ground **turmeric**
1 teaspoon (5 mL) **yellow mustard powder**
1 tablespoon (15 mL) **cumin seeds**
½ teaspoon (2 mL) **black peppercorns**
¼ teaspoon (1 mL) **Kashmiri chili powder**
½ teaspoon (2 mL) **cardamom seeds**
1 2-inch (5 cm) **cinnamon stick**
¼ teaspoon (1 mL) whole **cloves**

1 Combine the coriander seeds, turmeric, mustard powder, cumin seeds, peppercorns, chili powder, cardamom seeds, cinnamon stick and cloves in a dry skillet over medium heat. Toast, shaking the pan, for about 2 minutes, until fragrant. Transfer the mixture to a spice grinder and grind to a powder. Use immediately or store in a cool, dry place for up to 2 months.

GARAM MASALA

Garam masala is a warm spice blend filled with baking spices. It's a great example of an Indian spice blend that is not spicy-hot.

MAKES ¼ CUP (60 ML)

Coffee/spice grinder

2 tablespoons (30 mL) **cumin seeds**
1 tablespoon (15 mL) **cardamom seeds**
1 tablespoon (15 mL) **coriander seeds**
1 teaspoon (5 mL) freshly ground **black pepper**
2 teaspoons (10 mL) ground **cinnamon**
½ teaspoon (2 mL) ground **cloves**
½ teaspoon (2 mL) ground **nutmeg**

1 Combine the cumin seeds, cardamom seeds, coriander seeds, pepper, cinnamon, cloves and nutmeg in a dry skillet over medium heat. Toast, shaking the pan, for about 1 to 2 minutes, until fragrant. Transfer the mixture to a spice grinder and grind to a powder. Use immediately or store in a cool, dry place for up to 2 months.

CHAAT MASALA

Think of chaat masala as a powdered spice version of what happens when you squeeze a lemon over your food. It's a tart blend that's often shaken over fruit and snacks—the flavor wakes everything up.

MAKES ¼ CUP (60 ML)

Coffee/spice grinder

1½ tablespoons (22 mL) **cumin seeds**
1½ teaspoons (7 mL) **coriander seeds**
1 teaspoon (5 mL) **fennel seeds**
1 teaspoon (5 mL) **black peppercorns**
1½ tablespoons (22 mL) **amchur powder**
1½ tablespoons (22 mL) **kosher salt**
Pinch **asafoetida**
1 teaspoon (5 mL) dried **mint leaves**
1 teaspoon (5 mL) **ajwain seeds**
½ teaspoon (2 mL) ground **ginger**

1   Combine the cumin seeds, coriander seeds, fennel seeds and peppercorns in a dry skillet over medium heat. Toast, shaking the pan, for about 1 to 2 minutes, until fragrant. Add the amchur, salt, asafoetida, mint, ajwain seeds and ginger; toast for an additional 1 minute, until fragrant. Transfer the mixture to a spice grinder and grind to a powder. Use immediately or store in a cool, dry place for up to 2 months.

PANCH PHORON

India's answer to Everything Bagel Spice is panch phoron, a Bengali spice blend that combines whole seeds. I like to sprinkle it over breads and vegetables after they are cooked.

MAKES ¼ CUP (60 ML)

1 tablespoon (15 mL) **cumin seeds**
1 tablespoon (15 mL) **brown** or **yellow mustard seeds**
1 tablespoon (15 mL) **nigella seeds**
1 tablespoon (15 mL) **fennel seeds**
1 teaspoon (5 mL) **fenugreek seeds**

1 Combine the cumin seeds, mustard seeds, nigella seeds, fennel seeds and fenugreek seeds in a dry skillet over medium heat. Toast, shaking the pan, for about 1 to 2 minutes, until fragrant. Use the spices immediately or store in a cool, dry place for up to 2 months.

SRI LANKAN CURRY POWDER

When you want a spice blend that is full of color and floral notes and is also spicy-hot, turn to Sri Lankan curry powder.

MAKES ¼ CUP (60 ML)

Coffee/spice grinder

1½ tablespoons (22 mL) **coriander seeds**
1 tablespoon (15 mL) **cumin seeds**
2 teaspoons (10 mL) uncooked **white basmati rice**
1 tablespoon (15 mL) **black peppercorns**
1 tablespoon (15 mL) **fennel seeds**
1 teaspoon (5 mL) ground **fenugreek**
1 teaspoon (5 mL) ground **turmeric**
1 teaspoon (5 mL) ground **cardamom**
4 **dried red chiles**, torn into pieces

1 Combine the coriander seeds, cumin seeds, rice, peppercorns and fennel seeds in a dry skillet over medium heat. Toast, shaking the pan, for about 1 to 2 minutes, until fragrant. Add the fenugreek, turmeric, cardamom and chiles; toast for 1 minute, until fragrant. Transfer the mixture to a spice grinder and grind to a powder. Use immediately or store in a cool, dry place for up to 2 months.

BAFAT SPICE POWDER

Bafat spice powder comes from Mangalore, on the southeastern coast of India. That part of India was once colonized by the Portuguese, and you can still see their influence in the spices and cooking. This blend is rich and savory, with plenty of heat.

MAKES ½ CUP (125 ML)

Coffee/spice grinder

20 **dried red chiles**
¼ cup (60 mL) **coriander seeds**
2 tablespoons (30 mL) **cumin seeds**
1 teaspoon (5 mL) whole **cloves**
2 teaspoons (10 mL) **black peppercorns**
2 2-inch (5 cm) **cinnamon sticks**

1 Combine the chiles, coriander seeds, cumin seeds, cloves, peppercorns and cinnamon sticks in a dry skillet over medium heat. Toast, shaking the pan, for about 1 minute, until fragrant. Transfer the mixture to a spice grinder and grind to a powder. Use immediately or store in a cool, dry place for up to 2 months.

OTHER INGREDIENTS IN
MY INDIAN PANTRY

DRIED RED CHILES—I use dried red Thai bird chiles in my cooking, but if you can't find them, use arbol chiles or dried cayenne peppers.

CHICKPEAS are widely available both dried and canned. Before cooking dried chickpeas, pick them over to remove any pebbles or pieces of debris that may have gotten into the mix, then rinse in water.

COCONUT FLAKES (UNSWEETENED) are made from grated coconut that has been dried; it's sometimes called desiccated coconut. Don't confuse this with the sweetened coconut shreds used to decorate Easter cakes. The unsweetened flakes can be substituted for freshly grated or frozen coconut; just soak them in coconut milk or water for 30 minutes, then drain before using. For the recipes in this book, you just add the dry coconut flakes straight to the inner pot. The moist cooking environment of the Instant Pot means you don't need to worry about rehydrating them before cooking. If you are toasting coconut flakes, heat a toaster oven or oven to 325°F (160°C). Toast for 5 to 10 minutes, shaking the pan occasionally, so they toast evenly. You want them to be nicely golden brown and fragrant.

COCONUT MILK is a big part of South Indian cooking. Look for full-fat coconut milk, typically in cans or Tetra Paks—reduced-fat coconut milk just doesn't have the creaminess we need for coconut curries. And don't use coconut milk drinks, coconut water or coconut cream; those are not the same. Feel free to substitute full-fat coconut milk for the heavy or whipping (35%) cream in any recipe in this book.

Oh, CURRY LEAVES! I'd love to tell you that you could substitute something as easily accessible as bay leaves instead and the food would taste the same—but you just can't (shakes fist at the sky). Nothing else has their flavor. I don't like dried curry leaves (they just smell like dust) and always cook with fresh ones. If fresh curry leaves are hard to find where you live, buy more than you need from your local Indian grocery store or online and throw the extra sprigs into the freezer to keep as an emergency stash. It isn't a perfect solution, but is good insurance for when the Indian grocery is out of them.

DAL AND LENTILS—I've devoted a whole chapter to these pulses, so you better believe they're important. Dal are split versions of some types of lentils, and both dal and lentils are used extensively in Indian cooking. In this book I use chana dal, masoor dal, moong beans, and toor dal most often. Dal and lentils are toasted, ground and cooked whole, serving as a filling source of protein for vegetarians and meat eaters alike.

GINGER is key to Indian cooking. I wish there was an easier way to peel and mince it. I've tried the bottled ginger pastes and they just don't compare; the added preservatives change the flavor completely. I use the edge of a spoon to scrape off the skin (you can even scrape those nubs off as well) and then slice it to break up the fibers before putting it in a food processor. (My mini food processor gets a real workout puréeing ginger and garlic, so it's worth buying one if you do that a lot.)

GHEE is clarified butter that has been cooked a little longer so that the milk solids are toasted a bit before they are strained out, giving it a deeper flavor. You can buy ghee in Indian groceries and grocery stores that cater to healthy diets, or (ahem) make your own with the recipe on page 39. If you can't find ghee or want a vegan option, use vegetable oil or coconut oil.

JAGGERY looks like brown sugar and is made from either palm or cane sugar. Less sweet than brown sugar, it's sold in blocks or powdered form (I prefer powdered jaggery, as it's easier to measure). Brown sugar makes a good substitute if you can't get it.

LEMON AND LIME JUICE should always be fresh—no excuses. Lemons and limes last for a few weeks in the refrigerator, or you can squeeze out the juice and freeze it in ice-cube trays.

MAKRUT LIME LEAVES come from Asian limes and are among the best things you will ever smell. They are often labeled "kaffir lime leaves," but since *kaffir* is a racial slur in parts of the world, many chefs and grocery stores are now calling them makrut. Try to find them in Asian grocery stores; it's worth the extra effort. I usually buy extra to keep in my freezer just in case. If you can't find them, you can substitute 1 teaspoon (5 mL) grated lime zest; it won't taste the same, but you will get some of the citrus flavor you're looking for.

CARDAMOM

CHICKPEAS

KOKUM

LENTILS

DRIED
RED CHILES

POMEGRANATE

CURRY
LEAVES

GROUND
TURMERIC

MEATS are generally braised when cooked in the Instant Pot. You'll get much better results from dark-meat rather than white-meat poultry, and cuts of pork, lamb and beef like the shoulder and leg rather than the loin and filet, which can dry out, even when cooked in liquid.

NUTS are another key ingredient in Indian cooking. You'll find a lot of cashews, peanuts and pistachios in this book, and they often need to be toasted. You can toast nuts in an oven or on the stove, but I prefer the oven; the nuts get more evenly toasted that way, as opposed to being half raw with a few dark brown spots. I toast nuts in a toaster oven or regular oven heated to 350°F (180°C). Nuts will toast within 5 to 10 minutes, so you have to keep checking them, shaking the pan occasionally so that they toast evenly. You want them to be nicely golden brown and fragrant.

If you are toasting nuts in a skillet, do so over medium heat, shaking the pan frequently to prevent the nuts from burning in spots, for about 5 minutes, until they are nicely golden brown and fragrant. Immediately transfer them to a bowl to stop the cooking. Regardless of how you toast your nuts, don't forget about them! (I've thrown out pounds of burned nuts, which is an expensive way to learn this lesson.) I was taught in culinary school to place a nut on my cutting board while chopping onions or garlic, as a reminder that I had nuts toasting. It works!

PANEER is a fresh cheese that you can easily make at home (hint: see pages 64 to 73). But sometimes you need to buy it. And then sometimes you can't find it in stores. If you want a substitute for firm paneer, go with haloumi or *queso de freír*, which is a Mexican white cheese that, like haloumi and paneer, can withstand frying without melting. You can even use firm tofu. If you want a substitute for soft, gooey paneer, use fresh ricotta (full-fat, please!) or goat cheese. You can use paneer as a substitute for chicken in the recipes in this book.

RICE is the base of many Indian meals, especially those from South India, where rice is cultivated. There are tons of different varieties of rice out there, some long-grain, some fragrant, some short-grain and especially starchy, some brown, some white. Basmati and jasmine rice are the two most popular varieties used in Indian cooking and both are readily available. I often soak basmati rice for about 20 minutes before rinsing and cooking, which rids it of excess starch and elongates the grains. Jasmine rice is slightly shorter and starchier and just needs a quick rinse. I use white basmati rice almost exclusively in this book, although jasmine works well in Yogurt Rice (page 167) and both rice pudding desserts (pages 274 and 276). Although generally you can substitute brown basmati rice for white basmati in recipes—just make sure to change the cooking time from 4 minutes on high pressure to 22 minutes on high pressure—most of the biryanis and dishes with vegetables, meat, seafood and lentils are designed for white basmati only; the other ingredients would overcook in the time it takes for brown rice to cook.

SALT is another backbone ingredient. Throughout the book I call for kosher salt, and this is your official hint (okay, demand) to pay attention. The crystals in kosher salt are larger than in table salt, so 1 teaspoon (5 mL) of table salt is equal to almost twice the amount of kosher salt. Even within the category of kosher salts there are differences. Take, for example, Diamond Crystal salt and Morton salt; the Diamond Crystal crystals are larger than those in Morton salt (almost twice as large). I used Morton salt for the recipes in this book, since it is more widely available. As a general rule, 1 teaspoon (5 mL) table salt is roughly equivalent to 1¼ teaspoons (6 mL) Morton salt and 1¾ teaspoons (8 mL) Diamond Crystal salt. When in doubt, stay on the safe side and use less salt than you think you need. You can always add more later.

SERRANO AND GREEN THAI CHILES are used regularly in the book, but I want to remind you that chiles vary in heat level from crop to crop, so a little taste test might be in order, or just go easy until you know. I consider myself in the middle of the road when it comes to spice tolerance—my mother, husband and friend Amy can eat much spicier food than I—so I was fairly conservative about the amount of chiles used in the book. But you do you. If you are nervous about heat or have a low spice tolerance, cut back on the amount of fresh, dried or ground chiles in the dish. You can always add more but it's almost impossible to backtrack; you'll wind up drowning your food in yogurt and rice as you wipe the tears from your eyes. It's not a good look.

TAMARIND is a tart, sour dried fruit that is sold in block, paste or concentrate form. I find the concentrate the easiest to use—you don't have to soak it first and it measures easily.

YOGURT is another essential in the Indian kitchen. I teach you how to make your own yogurt on page 40, but when I want to buy it, I go with full-fat plain yogurt or Greek yogurt, preferably 2% or whole. The thick texture means that it doesn't get too thin when watered down with citrus juice or other ingredients in raita. Even better, in marinades it clings to meats, tenderizing them gently but effectively in a short amount of time. For lassis, thinner yogurt is fine. Just don't use skim milk or 0% yogurt—they lack the richness we want in these dishes.

HOW TO USE THIS BOOK

This book was written and designed for people who are curious about cooking Indian food, whether it is part of their heritage or simply the type of food they like to eat — or want to start eating! I have written it for people across all levels of expertise. If you are an Instant Pot newbie, you'll find cooking instructions spelled out for you as clearly as possible. And if you are an expert, I hope you'll learn some lesser-known tricks and uses for your Instant Pot, to help you get the most out of cooking with it.

For each recipe, start by looking at the row of cooking functions across the top of the page. That list will explain which Instant Pot cooking functions you will use to cook that dish and how long each will take. Keep in mind this list does not include oven or stovetop cooking. I've included the amount of time needed for the machine to come to pressure and to release pressure for each recipe, so you can accurately plan (because no one likes a 30-minute meal that actually takes almost an hour to prepare). The total time also includes any out-of-Instant Pot preparation like blending or stovetop or oven cooking.

When you look at each recipe, check above the ingredient list to see if there are any special pieces of equipment that you will need, such as a food processor or coffee/spice grinder. You'll find icons around the recipe title that identify which recipes are gluten-free **GF**, vegetarian **VEG**, and vegan **V**, if those are considerations for you. There are a lot of options in this book that fit all of these dietary requirements.

I've done everything I can to make cooking Indian food in the Instant Pot as unintimidating as possible. So let's get started!

CHAPTER ONE

Ghee
YOGURT
and
CHEESE

SAUTÉ
9 MIN

 TOTAL
10 MIN

 MAKES
1½ CUPS
(375 ML)

GHEE

VEG **GF**

Ghee is the liquid gold of Indian kitchens. More than just melted butter, ghee is butter cooked until the milk solids have sunk to the bottom of the pot and begun to caramelize, giving the butterfat a full, toasty flavor and golden color. You then strain off the butterfat, which means you can cook with it over high heat without its smoking or burning like regular butter. It's also shelf-stable, so it does not have to be refrigerated. Usually you have to stand over a pot of ghee to make sure it doesn't start to brown, but with the Instant Pot, you can walk away from the bubbling mixture for most of the cooking time. Make sure to use a high-quality unsalted butter when you make ghee; you can't make gold from the cheap stuff.

1   pound (500 g) **unsalted butter**, quartered

1   Place the butter in the inner pot and, using the Sauté function on Normal, heat until melted. (The butter will sputter a bit as the water content cooks off and then it will foam up, so don't be alarmed.) Cook the butter for about 7 minutes, keeping an eye on the inner pot for the last few minutes of cooking, until golden. Be careful not to cook the butter beyond a pale brown color (brown butter is delicious, but more toasted than what we're aiming for here).

2   Pour the ghee through a fine-mesh sieve lined with cheesecloth, a coffee filter or an unbleached paper towel, set over a bowl. (Don't toss out all those milk solids at the bottom of your pot! They are delicious mixed into rice, spread on toast or spooned over cooked vegetables.) Let cool to room temperature, then transfer to an airtight container and store in a cool, dry place for up to 3 months.

NOTE *You can season your ghee if you'd like to give it a bit of flavor. Just add a pinch of saffron, crushed chile, toasted cardamom or cumin seeds to your ghee after straining it. I like to drizzle spiced ghee over rice to give it a little extra oomph.*

YOGURT
8 HR 25 MIN

SAUTÉ
5 MIN

TOTAL
40 MIN
(PLUS 8 HR
INACTIVE TIME)

MAKES
6 CUPS
(1.5 L)

PLAIN YOGURT

VEG GF

When my parents moved to America in 1969, it was almost impossible to find plain yogurt. Stores carried only saccharine-sweet "fruit" yogurt dyed a shade of pink not found in nature. My mom bought a yogurt maker and kept it running regularly so she could make plain yogurt for our family. These days, plain yogurt is everywhere, but I like making my own. It's very easy—all you need is milk and a little yogurt with active bacterial cultures to use as your starter (it's like sourdough starter for making bread) and then set the yogurt to cook overnight. For me, homemade yogurt is delicious and personal; it reminds me of my mom negotiating her way in a new country.

8   cups (2 L) **whole milk**
2   tablespoons (30 mL) **plain yogurt**

1   Pour the milk into the inner pot, secure the lid and select the Yogurt function on More. Heat for about 25 minutes, until the display reads "Yogt."

2   Remove the lid. Using the Sauté function on Low, simmer the milk for an additional 5 minutes (you will need to set a separate timer for this step).

3   Remove the inner pot from the Instant Pot, then place it in a large bowl half-filled with ice water. Cool, stirring occasionally, for about 10 minutes, until the temperature of the milk drops to 115°F (46°C) on an instant-read thermometer.

4   Ladle 1 cup (250 mL) warm milk into a small bowl and whisk in the yogurt. Return the mixture to the inner pot and stir to combine.

5   Wipe the exterior of the inner pot dry, then place the inner pot back in the Instant Pot, secure the lid and set the pressure valve to Venting. Using the Yogurt function on Normal, ferment the yogurt for 8 hours (I've let mine ferment for up to 12 hours with no problems).

6   Transfer the yogurt to an airtight container and refrigerate for at least 6 hours before serving. It will keep in the refrigerator for up to 1 week.

NOTE   *If you want to make thicker, Greek-style yogurt, ladle the finished yogurt into a fine-mesh sieve lined with cheesecloth, a coffee filter or an unbleached paper towel, placed over a large bowl, and strain it in the refrigerator for 3 hours.*

YOGURT
18 HR 25 MIN

TOTAL
1 HR
(PLUS APPROX.
18 HR INACTIVE
TIME)

MAKES
3²/₃ CUPS
(900 ML)

(VEG) (GF) (V) COCONUT MILK
YOGURT

If you follow a vegan or dairy-free diet, this yogurt is for you. You can use coconut yogurt in place of dairy yogurt throughout the book, without any problems. Although coconut yogurt is thinner than thick, Greek-style yogurt, it's fantastic in raitas and lassis. As with dairy yogurt, you'll need a little yogurt with active bacterial cultures to make this recipe; check the label of your coconut yogurt to make sure it has active cultures.

2   cans (each 14 oz/398 mL) full-fat **coconut milk**

2   tablespoons (30 mL) **coconut milk yogurt**

1   Pour the coconut milk and coconut milk yogurt into the inner pot and whisk until combined.

2   Secure the lid and select the Yogurt function on More. Heat for about 25 minutes, until the display reads "Yogt." Remove the lid and turn off the Instant Pot. Let stand, whisking occasionally, until the temperature drops to 115°F (46°C) on an instant-read thermometer.

3   Secure the lid, set the pressure valve to Venting and, using the Yogurt function on Normal, ferment the yogurt for 18 hours (I've let mine ferment for up to 22 hours with no problems).

4   Transfer the yogurt to an airtight container and refrigerate until serving. The yogurt will keep in the refrigerator for up to 1 week.

NOTE *If you want to thicken your coconut milk yogurt, whisk 1 teaspoon (5 mL) powdered gelatin or agar-agar into the coconut milk in Step 3 before setting it to ferment.*

LASSIS

Lassis are essentially the smoothies of India. They were
first created in Punjab, in the northern part of the country, and can
be either sweet and savory. I think lassis make a great breakfast,
but they are typically drunk after spicy meals to soothe the
stomach. You can use regular plain yogurt or thick Greek yogurt
to make lassis.

MANGO LIME
VEG GF ROSEWATER
LASSI

Mango lassis are everywhere these days. It's almost impossible to get the fresh, ripe Alphonso mangos that make lassis in India so delicious, so I use canned mango purée here, but use fresh if you prefer. The lime juice and rosewater wake it up and brighten the flavor, but if you can't find rosewater, try cherry juice or puréed strawberries instead.

Blender

- 2 cups (500 mL) **Plain Yogurt** (page 40) or store-bought
- 1 cup (250 mL) **mango purée**
- ¼ cup (60 mL) **water** or **whey** (approx.)
- 1 tablespoon (15 mL) **granulated sugar** (approx.)
- 2 teaspoons (10 mL) freshly squeezed **lime juice** (approx.)
- ½ teaspoon (2 mL) **rosewater** or **cherry juice**

1 Combine the yogurt, mango, water, sugar, lime juice and rosewater in a blender; blend on high speed until smooth and creamy.

2 Taste and add additional water if needed; you want this to be creamy but thin enough to drink. Add more lime juice for acidity or sugar for sweetness, if you prefer. Pour into 2 glasses and serve.

NOTE *When I made this for my friend Christine, she said the creamy texture reminded her of zabaglione, the delicious custardy Italian dessert, and suggested I serve this with cake. If you want to take her advice (Christine's a pretty amazing chef, so I usually do what she says), spoon some of this lassi over fruit salad, or serve it alongside fruit and a light cake like angel food cake.*

Banana CARDAMOM VEG GF LASSI

This lassi is so creamy and sweet that it feels more like a breakfast or dessert lassi to me. It's also very popular with my friends' kids. When I make this lassi, I like to use up some of the frozen bananas that seem to constantly stack up in my freezer, but fresh will also work—the riper the better.

Blender

2 cups (500 mL) **Plain Yogurt** (page 40) or store-bought

4 small **bananas**, ripe or overripe or frozen, sliced

2 tablespoons (30 mL) **honey** (approx.)

1 teaspoon (5 mL) minced **ginger**

½ teaspoon (2 mL) ground **cardamom**, toasted

Water (optional)

1 Combine the yogurt, bananas, honey, ginger and cardamom in a blender; blend on high speed until smooth and creamy.

2 Taste and add water if needed; you want this to be creamy but thin enough to drink. Sweeten with more honey, if you prefer. Pour into 2 glasses and serve.

VEG GF GINGER TURMERIC
LASSI

This is a take on *haldi ka doodh*, the classic drink that Indian parents give their children when they aren't feeling well. Turmeric drinks have now become trendy, which validates what Indians have been saying for years. I like to make this when I am feeling run down. I can hear generations of aunties telling me I need to drink it.

Blender

- 2 cups (500 mL) **Plain Yogurt** (page 40) or store-bought
- 2 tablespoons (30 mL) **honey** (approx.)
- 2 teaspoons (10 mL) minced **ginger**
- 3 teaspoons (15 mL) freshly squeezed **lemon juice** (approx.)
- 2 teaspoons (10 mL) ground **turmeric**
  Water (optional)

1 Combine the yogurt, honey, ginger, lemon juice and turmeric in a blender; blend on high speed until smooth and creamy.

2 Taste and add water if needed; you want this to be creamy but thin enough to drink. Add more lemon juice for acidity or honey for sweetness, if you prefer. Pour into 2 glasses and serve.

PREP
5 MIN

TOTAL
7 MIN

SERVES
2

Salt Lime LASSI

VEG GF

Lassis aren't always sweet! This salt lime lassi, which is especially popular in the southern parts of India, is more refreshing than a sugary soft drink on a hot, humid summer afternoon.

Blender

- 2 cups (500 mL) **Plain Yogurt** (page 40) or store-bought
- ¼ cup (60 mL) fresh **mint** leaves
- ¼ cup (60 mL) freshly squeezed **lime juice** (approx.)
- ¼ cup (60 mL) cold **water**
- ¼ teaspoon (1 mL) **kosher salt**
- Pinch ground **cumin**

1 Combine the yogurt, mint, lime juice, water, salt and cumin in a blender; blend on high speed until smooth and creamy.

2 Taste and add water if needed; you want this to be creamy but thin enough to drink. Add more lime juice if you want it to taste a little more tart. Pour into 2 glasses and serve.

STRAWBERRY
·LIME
VEG · GF
LASSI

This is a nice, bright lassi that is especially tasty in the spring, when strawberries and mint are in season. Make sure you toast the fennel seeds before grinding them; it brings out their flavor. I love how rosewater makes the strawberries taste even fruitier, but if you can't find it, use cherry juice instead.

1 Combine the strawberries, yogurt, lime juice, mint, ground fennel and rosewater (if using) in a blender; blend on high speed until smooth and creamy.

2 Taste and add water if needed; you want this to be creamy but thin enough to drink. Sweeten with sugar, if you prefer. Pour into 2 glasses and serve.

Blender

1 pound (500 g) **strawberries**, chopped

2 cups (500 mL) **Plain Yogurt** (page 40) or store-bought

¼ cup (60 mL) freshly squeezed **lime juice**

¼ cup (60 mL) fresh **mint** leaves

1 teaspoon (5 mL) **fennel seeds**, toasted and ground (page 20)

1 teaspoon (5 mL) **rosewater** or **cherry juice** (optional)

   Water (optional)

   Granulated sugar (optional)

CHAI Lassi

The warm spices in chai make this lassi feel especially right in fall and winter. If you are of the pumpkin spice latte persuasion, add 1 cup (250 mL) canned pumpkin purée to the mix.

Blender

2 cups (500 mL) **Plain Yogurt** (page 40) or store-bought

1 cup (250 mL) strong brewed **chai**, cooled to room temperature

1 teaspoon (5 mL) **vanilla extract**

½ teaspoon (2 mL) ground **cinnamon**

1 teaspoon (5 mL) **jaggery** or **brown sugar** (approx.)

Water (optional)

1   Combine the yogurt, chai, vanilla, cinnamon and jaggery in a blender; blend on high speed until smooth and creamy.

2   Taste and add water if needed; you want this to be creamy but thin enough to drink. Add more jaggery for sweetness, if you prefer. Pour into 2 glasses and serve.

VEG GF Cucumber RAITA

I think I ate gallons of cucumber raita when I was a kid, because it saved me when I ate my mom's extra-spicy Indian food. (Ironically, my Irish mother has the spiciest palate of anyone in my family. Go figure.) But when I went to college and had my first gyro with tzatziki sauce, I quickly realized that the love of a good yogurt sauce is universal. I use Kirby or English cucumbers for my raita because their very thin skins and small seeds are easier to eat. Regular cucumbers are fine too, but make sure to peel them and scoop out the seeds.

2 cups (500 mL) **Plain Yogurt** (page 40) or store-bought

1 medium **English cucumber** or 2 **Kirby cucumbers**, finely chopped or grated

½ cup (125 mL) minced **red onion**

¼ cup (60 mL) minced fresh **cilantro**

2 **garlic cloves**, grated

1 tablespoon (15 mL) minced fresh **mint** leaves

1 tablespoon (15 mL) freshly squeezed **lime juice**

1 tablespoon (15 mL) **vegetable oil**

1 teaspoon (5 mL) **mustard seeds**

½ teaspoon (2 mL) ground **cumin**

½ teaspoon (2 mL) **kosher salt**

1 Combine the yogurt, cucumber, onion, cilantro, garlic, mint and lime juice in a medium bowl.

2 Heat the vegetable oil in a small skillet over medium heat. Add the mustard seeds, cumin and salt and cook for about 1 minute, until the seeds begin to pop.

3 Transfer the raita to a serving bowl, pour the tempered spices overtop and serve.

NOTE *If you want to make this raita ahead of time, combine the ingredients in Step 1 up to 2 days in advance, cover and store in an airtight container in the refrigerator. When you're ready to serve, heat the oil, sizzle the spices and pour them over the raita.*

PREP
15 MIN

TOTAL
15 MIN

MAKES
2½ CUPS
(625 ML)

POMEGRANATE
RAITA

Pomegranates show up in late fall and winter, offering their gorgeous red seeds full of tart flavor. This raita cools you off while adding unexpected pops of tart juice and color—it's like eating a bowl of rubies. I like to serve this with Kerala Chicken Curry (page 208); the extra acid from the pomegranate seeds brightens the flavors nicely.

2 cups (500 mL) **Plain Yogurt** (page 40) or store-bought

¾ cup (175 mL) **pomegranate seeds**

½ cup (125 mL) minced fresh **cilantro**

4 **green onions**, minced

2 teaspoons (10 mL) freshly squeezed **lime juice**

½ teaspoon (2 mL) **kosher salt**

1 Combine the yogurt, pomegranate seeds, cilantro, green onions, lime juice and salt in a medium bowl. Serve immediately or store in an airtight container in the refrigerator for up to 4 days.

PREP	MANUAL	RELEASE	TOTAL	MAKES
3 MIN	**20 MIN**	**NATURAL/ QUICK**	**40 MIN**	**2½ CUPS** (625 ML)

Beet RAITA

VEG · GF

I like this raita for the color it adds to the table, as well as the earthy flavor you get from the beets. It goes well with Tea-Braised Lamb Stew (page 222) and is especially tasty as a dip for carrots and other veggies. Just don't wear a white shirt while peeling and chopping the beets, and wash your hands immediately after handling so you don't dye them pink.

Instant Pot trivet
Food processor or blender

2	small **beets**, trimmed
1	cup (250 mL) **water**
½	teaspoon (2 mL) ground **cumin**
½	teaspoon (2 mL) **kosher salt**
2	cups (500 mL) **Plain Yogurt** (page 40) or store-bought
2	teaspoons (10 mL) **vegetable oil**
6	fresh **curry leaves**, torn into pieces

1 Place the beets on a trivet in the inner pot. Add the water. Secure the lid and cook on high pressure for 20 minutes (add about 3 minutes to the cook time if the beets are large).

2 Once the cooking is complete, let the pressure release naturally for 10 minutes, then quick-release the remaining pressure. Check to make sure the beets are tender. If necessary, cook on high pressure for an additional 3 minutes.

3 Remove the beets from the inner pot and place in a medium bowl. Let cool until just warm, then peel and cut into large chunks.

4 Combine the beets, cumin and salt in a food processor; process until completely smooth.

5 Whisk together the beet mixture and the yogurt in a serving bowl.

6 Heat the vegetable oil in a small skillet over medium heat. Add the curry leaves and cook for about 2 minutes, until slightly frizzled.

7 Pour the tempered oil and curry leaves over the raita; serve.

NOTE *If you want to make this raita ahead of time, follow the recipe to the end of Step 5 up to 4 days in advance, cover and store in an airtight container in the refrigerator. When you're ready to serve, heat the oil, sizzle the curry leaves and pour them over the raita.*

PREP
5 MIN

TOTAL
15 MIN

MAKES
2 CUPS
(500 ML)

VEG GF *Cucumber Raita* SOUP

This soup will save you on one of those hot, sultry days when the idea of eating just about anything is draining but you are still (maddeningly) hungry. I like it on its own for lunch, or with salad and grilled chicken for dinner.

Blender

- 1   teaspoon (5 mL) **coriander seeds**, toasted and ground (page 20)
- 1   teaspoon (5 mL) **cumin seeds**, toasted and ground
- 1   teaspoon (5 mL) **kosher salt** (approx.)
- 1   **English cucumber**, peeled, seeded and coarsely chopped
- ½   cup (125 mL) **buttermilk** or **whey**
- 2   cups (500 mL) **Plain Yogurt** (page 40) or store-bought

1   Combine the ground coriander, ground cumin, salt and cucumber in a blender; blend on high speed until smooth. Add the buttermilk and blend on high speed until smooth. Add the yogurt and blend on high speed until smooth and well combined. Taste the soup and add more salt, if desired. Serve immediately or store in an airtight container in the refrigerator for up to 8 hours.

PREP
5 MIN

TOTAL
15 MIN

MAKES
2½ CUPS
(625 ML)

LEMONY ONION VEG GF RAITA

I like to serve this raita with Butter Chicken with Spiced Cashews (page 206), scoop it over a bowl of chickpeas with fresh greens for lunch, or use it to accompany any spicy-hot food such as Lamb Vindaloo Samosas (page 104). It's very simple but so refreshing.

1 small **onion**, minced

½ cup (125 mL) freshly squeezed **lemon juice**

2 cups (500 mL) **Plain Yogurt** (page 40) or store-bought

1 teaspoon (5 mL) **fennel seeds**, toasted and crushed (page 20)

1 Combine the onion and lemon juice in a medium bowl; let stand for 10 minutes.

2 Stir in the yogurt and crushed fennel seeds. Serve immediately or store in an airtight container in the refrigerator for up to 4 days.

PANEER

Paneer is a fresh cheese that is eaten widely in India in curries or fried and served on its own. It's also one of the easiest things in the world to make. I learned to make it with milk, but after a lot of experimenting (and paneer eating, because I'll do that), I've come to prefer using a combination of whole milk and cream.

YOU CAN USE ANY ACID to curdle the milk, but plain white vinegar is the most reliable. You can also make paneer to the texture you want: firm and somewhat bouncy to the touch (like firm tofu) or soft, like ricotta. Both types of paneer should be used within 5 days of making it, but firm paneer can be frozen for up to 2 months.

Regardless of whether you make firm or soft paneer, you'll end up with a few cups of whey (the liquid byproduct) after making it. It's full of protein, freezes well and has a tangy flavor that works in other recipes from soup to bread. Here are a few things you can do with whey:

- Swap it in for water when making bread dough, to add a slight tang to the bread.

- Use it to thin lassis and smoothies.

- Soak nuts in it.

- Use it in a marinade (the lactic acid helps tenderize meat).

- Swap it for stock in soups — especially creamy soups.

- Make oatmeal, porridge or congee with it.

- Cook rice or other grains in it.

- Mix it with milk to create a substitute for buttermilk in baking.

- Use it as a brine for meat or cheese.

VEG GF SOFT PANEER

Sometimes you want a softer paneer, one that you can spoon over a bowl of Chana Masala (page 198), use as the base for Rasmalai Cake (page 262) or smear onto pieces of Naan (page 252). I like to toast cumin and mustard seeds with Kashmiri chili powder in oil, drizzle the mixture over soft paneer and serve the resulting dip with naan or roti as a snack. Or you can always eat it straight with a spoon while standing over the sink —it's that good.

4 cups (1 L) **whole milk**

1 cup (250 mL) **heavy** or **whipping** (35%) **cream**

1 teaspoon (5 mL) **kosher salt**

3 tablespoons (45 mL) **white vinegar**

1 Combine the milk, cream and salt in the inner pot. Using the Sauté function on High, heat the mixture for about 5 minutes, until simmering.

2 Add the vinegar. Secure the lid and cook on high pressure for 4 minutes.

3 Once the cooking is complete, let the pressure release naturally for 10 minutes, then quick-release the remaining pressure.

4 Remove the lid and stir gently; the milk and cream will have separated into solid curds and translucent whey. (See page 65 for tips on how to use the leftover whey.)

5 Place a fine-mesh sieve lined with cheesecloth, a coffee filter or an unbleached paper towel over a large bowl. Ladle the curds into the lined sieve. Let stand for at least 15 minutes or up to 1 hour. Check its consistency; you want it to resemble ricotta cheese. If the paneer has thickened too much for your taste, stir a little whey back into it (or cream, if you're feeling decadent—no judgment here). Discard the cheesecloth. Serve immediately or transfer to an airtight container in the refrigerator for up to 1 week.

VEG GF FIRM PANEER

This firm paneer is a little softer in texture than what you find in Indian grocery stores, but it can still be cubed and fried for dishes such as Fried Chili Paneer (page 113) and Vegetable Paneer Biryani (page 176).

Cheesecloth

4	cups (1 L)	**whole milk**
1	cup (250 mL)	**half-and-half** (10%) **cream**
3	tablespoons (45 mL)	**white vinegar**
1	teaspoon (5 mL)	**kosher salt**

NOTE *You can up your paneer game by buying a tofu press, which comes with a straining cloth. It will make the process of pressing easier and will give you a perfectly square block of paneer.*

1   Combine the milk, cream, vinegar and salt in the inner pot. Using the Sauté function on High, heat the mixture for about 5 minutes, until simmering.

2   Secure the lid and cook on high pressure for 5 minutes.

3   Once the cooking is complete, let the pressure release naturally for 10 minutes, then quick-release the remaining pressure.

4   Remove the lid and stir gently; the milk and cream will have separated into solid curds and translucent whey. (See page 65 for tips on how to use the leftover whey.)

5   Place a fine-mesh sieve lined with cheesecloth over a large bowl. Ladle the curds into the lined sieve, let drain for 1 minute, then gather up the sides of the cheesecloth and twist to press out the excess liquid. Place the cheesecloth package on a rimmed plate and put a weight on top (I use a large can of tomatoes or beans).

6   Transfer the plate, package and weight to the refrigerator to firm up for at least 8 hours or up to 24 hours. (The longer you can keep the paneer in the refrigerator to firm up, the less likely it is to crumble when sliced.) Pour off any accumulated whey and discard the cheesecloth. Serve immediately or store in an airtight container in the refrigerator for up to 1 week.

PREP	SAUTÉ	MANUAL	RELEASE	TOTAL	MAKES
10 MIN	**5 MIN**	**5 MIN**	**NATURAL/ QUICK**	**30 MIN** (PLUS 8 HR INACTIVE TIME)	**1½ CUPS** (375 ML) OR **9 OUNCES** (275 G)

CORIANDER
VEG GF *Black Pepper*
PANEER

Firm paneer gets an extra boost of floral and peppery flavors from just-crushed coriander seeds and black peppercorns in this recipe. Adding lemon juice gives it a nice citrusy note. I like to use it in Saag Paneer (page 142) and Chana Masala (page 198).

Cheesecloth

4   cups (1 L) **whole milk**
1   cup (250 mL) **half-and-half** (10%) **cream**
1   tablespoon (15 mL) **black peppercorns**, crushed
1   tablespoon (15 mL) **coriander seeds**, crushed
1   tablespoon (15 mL) **kosher salt**
1   tablespoon (15 mL) **white vinegar**
⅓   cup (75 mL) freshly squeezed **lemon juice**

1   Combine the milk, cream, peppercorns, coriander seeds and salt in the inner pot. Using the Sauté function on High, heat for about 5 minutes, until simmering.

2   Add the vinegar and lemon juice. Secure the lid and cook on high pressure for 5 minutes.

3   Once the cooking is complete, let the pressure release naturally for 10 minutes, then quick-release the remaining pressure.

4   Remove the lid and stir gently; the milk and cream will have separated into solid curds and translucent whey. (See page 65 for tips on how to use the leftover whey.)

5   Place a fine-mesh sieve lined with cheesecloth over a large bowl. Ladle the curds into the lined sieve, let them drain for 1 minute, then gather up the sides of the cheesecloth and twist to press out the excess liquid. Place the cheesecloth package on a rimmed plate and put a weight on top (I use a large can of tomatoes or beans).

6   Transfer plate, package and weight to the refrigerator to firm up for at least 8 hours or up to 24 hours. (The longer you can keep the paneer in the refrigerator to firm up, the less likely it is to crumble.) Pour off any accumulated whey and discard the cheesecloth. Serve immediately or store in an airtight container in the refrigerator for up to 1 week.

VEG GF CILANTRO CHILE PANEER

I love this firm paneer in Vegetable Paneer Biryani (page 176) or Lentil Salad with Paneer and Tomatoes (page 193). It has loads of flavor and goes with just about anything.

Cheesecloth

4 cups (1 L) **whole milk**

1 cup (250 mL) **half-and-half** (10%) **cream**

2 tablespoons (30 mL) minced fresh **cilantro**

1 tablespoon (15 mL) crushed **dried red chiles**

1 tablespoon (15 mL) **kosher salt**

3 tablespoons (45 mL) **white vinegar**

1 Combine the milk, cream, cilantro, crushed chiles and salt in the inner pot. Using the Sauté function on High, heat for about 5 minutes, until simmering.

2 Add the vinegar. Secure the lid and cook on high pressure for 5 minutes.

3 Let the pressure release naturally for 10 minutes, then quick-release the remaining pressure.

4 Remove the lid and stir gently; the milk and cream will have separated into solid curds and translucent whey. (See page 65 for tips on how to use the leftover whey.)

5 Place a fine-mesh sieve lined with cheesecloth over a large bowl. Ladle the curds into the lined sieve, let drain for 1 minute, then gather up the sides of the cheesecloth and twist to press out the excess liquid. Place the cheesecloth package on a rimmed plate and put a weight on top (I use a large can of tomatoes or beans).

6 Transfer plate, package and weight to the refrigerator to firm up for at least 8 hours or up to 24 hours. (The longer you can keep the paneer in the refrigerator to firm up, the less likely it is to crumble.) Pour off any accumulated whey and discard the cheesecloth. Serve immediately or store in an airtight container in the refrigerator for up to 1 week.

SAFFRON HONEY VEG GF Paneer

Just like ricotta, paneer can be sweet or savory. Here's a soft version that skews toward dessert or breakfast territory, making it perfect for smearing on crackers or toast or dolloping on top of pancakes or French toast.

4 cups (1 L) **whole milk**

1 cup (250 mL) **heavy** or **whipping** (35%) **cream**

1 teaspoon (5 mL) **kosher salt**

Large pinch **saffron**

¼ cup (60 mL) **honey**

3 tablespoons (45 mL) **white vinegar**

1 Combine the milk, cream, salt and saffron in the inner pot. Using the Sauté function on High, heat the mixture for about 5 minutes, until simmering. Turn off the heat and let stand for 20 minutes, until the milk has turned golden yellow.

2 Using the Sauté function on High, heat the milk for about 3 minutes, until simmering again. Add the honey and stir until dissolved.

3 Add the vinegar. Secure the lid and cook on high pressure for 4 minutes.

4 Once the cooking is complete, let the pressure release naturally for 10 minutes, then quick-release the remaining pressure. Stir gently; the milk and cream will have separated into solid curds and translucent whey. (See page 65 for tips on how to use the leftover whey.)

5 Place a fine-mesh sieve lined with cheesecloth, a coffee filter or an unbleached paper towel over a large bowl. Ladle the curds into the lined sieve. Let stand for at least 15 minutes and up to 1 hour, depending on how thick you want it to be; I like it to resemble ricotta cheese. If the paneer has thickened too much for your taste, stir a little whey or cream back into it. Discard the cheesecloth. Serve immediately or store in an airtight container in the refrigerator up to 1 week.

CHAPTER TWO

PICKLES

and

CHUTNEYS

PREP
5 MIN

MANUAL
9 MIN

RELEASE
NATURAL

TOTAL
25 MIN
(PLUS 2 DAYS
INACTIVE TIME)

MAKES
2 CUPS
(500 ML)

(VEG) (GF) (V) SAFFRON-PRESERVED

MEYER LEMONS

Why am I asking you to seek out Meyer lemons? Because Meyer lemons are citrus magic, friends. It's like regular lemons and tangerines had a baby—a baby with a sweet citrusy flavor, a little acidity and a gorgeous orangey yellow skin (this kid is clearly the favorite). I get so excited when Meyer lemons make their appearance at the market in December that I buy as many as I can carry. Then I get home and, absent of any other plans, preserve them so I can enjoy their sunny flavor all year round. (That being said, you can use regular lemons here and it will still be delicious.) You'll find tons of ways to use these lemons: chop them up for a chutney, toss them with cooked rice to make Preserved Lemon Jeera Rice (page 163) or biryani, fold them into Apple Pomegranate Moong Dal Bowl (page 201) or blend them into a salad dressing.

Two 8-ounce (250 mL) canning jars

6   **Meyer lemons** or **lemons**
½   cup (125 mL) **kosher salt**, divided
2   teaspoons (10 mL) **cumin seeds**
2   teaspoons (10 mL) **nigella seeds**
     Large pinch **saffron**
4   **bay leaves**
1   cup (250 mL) **water**

1   Quarter the lemons lengthwise, cutting down to ½ inch (1 cm) from the bottom, so the quarters are still attached. Pack about 1 teaspoon (5 mL) salt between each lemon quarter.

2   Place the salted lemons, any remaining salt, cumin seeds, nigella seeds, saffron and bay leaves in the inner pot. Pour the water overtop. Secure the lid and cook on high pressure for 9 minutes.

3   Once the cooking is complete, let the pressure release naturally.

4   Divide the lemons between clean jars, packing them in tightly and leaving ½ inch (1 cm) headspace (it's okay to split the lemons in half if needed to fill the jars). Pour the cooking liquid (including the bay leaves and spices) over the lemons in each jar. Wipe the rims and seal the jars with the lids. Refrigerate for least 2 days or up to 1 year before using.

NOTES *When you are ready to use your preserved lemons, pull a segment or two out of the jar and give them a quick rinse under cold water before using. I like to use the entire lemon, rind and all—the rind will have mellowed to a nice soft texture.*

Once you've finished your preserved lemons, give the remaining tart brine a second life by using it instead of vinegar in salad dressings or drizzled over veggies, soups or grain salads.

CORIANDER LEMON
CHUTNEY

The light, floral flavors of coriander and Meyer lemons come together in this powerhouse chutney, which is reminiscent of an Italian salsa verde but with Indian soul. It really shows its worth when added to any soup, rice or dal that is a little *meh*. Stir this chutney into leftover chicken and rice when you have no idea what to eat, and you'll basically save dinner. I mix it into Coconut Chili Summer Vegetable Kootu (page 202) and Kolkata Biryani (page 184).

3 **Meyer lemons** or **lemons**, finely chopped
2 tablespoons (30 mL) minced **ginger**
1 tablespoon (15 mL) **coriander seeds**, crushed
½ cup (125 mL) **jaggery** or **brown sugar**
1 **garlic clove**, minced
1 **green Thai chile**, minced
¼ cup (60 mL) **apple cider vinegar**
¼ cup (60 mL) **water**

1 Combine the lemons, ginger, crushed coriander seeds, jaggery, garlic, chile, vinegar and water in the inner pot. Secure the lid and cook on high pressure for 9 minutes.

2 Once the cooking is complete, let the pressure release naturally.

3 Remove the lid and stir. Using the Sauté function on High, cook, stirring frequently, for about 3 minutes, until chutney has thickened slightly. Serve immediately or let cool and store in an airtight container in the refrigerator for up to 3 weeks.

CORIANDER VEG GF
CARAMELIZED ONION
CHUTNEY

Caramelized onions take a long time to cook on the stove, time that is made somewhat painful by the fact that they have to be watched and stirred almost constantly to make sure they don't burn instead of caramelizing. The Instant Pot is a lifesaver when it comes to easy, walk-away-from-the-stove-and-get-on-with-your-life caramelized onions. They get a boost of browning from the addition of baking soda, a tip I picked up from writer J. Kenji López-Alt on the Serious Eats website. His column—a must-read for anyone who wants to understand the hows and whys behind cooking—explains how baking soda increases the Maillard reaction, which is the browning that is so key to caramelized onions. It's a tip that makes these onions easy and less of a project. Adding coriander to the onions as they caramelize gives them a gentle citrusy, floral flavor that makes this chutney a winner.

- 5 tablespoons (75 mL) **unsalted butter**
- 2 pounds (1 kg) **onions**, very thinly sliced
- ½ teaspoon (2 mL) **baking soda**
- 1 teaspoon (5 mL) **kosher salt**
- 1 teaspoon (5 mL) freshly ground **black pepper**
- 2 teaspoon (10 mL) ground **coriander**

1 Using the Sauté function on Normal, melt the butter in the inner pot. Add the onions and baking soda; stir to combine. Add the salt, pepper and coriander; cook, stirring occasionally, for about 4 minutes, until the onions have softened.

2 Secure the lid and cook on high pressure for 18 minutes.

3 Once the cooking is complete, quick-release the pressure.

4 Remove the lid. Using the Sauté function on High, cook the onions for about 5 minutes, stirring frequently, until the liquid reduces and the onions are deep brown. Serve immediately or let cool and store in airtight containers in the refrigerator for up to 1 week.

NOTE *If you have extra chutney, you can store it in an airtight container in the freezer for up to 2 months.*

CAULIFLOWER CARROT PICKLE

VEG · GF · V

This is the kind of pickle that tends to hang out in the back of my fridge, emerging like a hero at just the right moment to perk up cheese platters, big, meaty sandwiches or a bowl of Rajasthani Panchmel Dal (page 197) and rice. Don't toss the pickling liquid when you are done with the vegetables; I spoon a bit of it into the cooking water for lentils or rice to lend a little extra punch.

- 2 tablespoons (30 mL) **vegetable oil**
- 4 **garlic cloves**, smashed
- 2 teaspoons (10 mL) **yellow mustard seeds**
- 2 teaspoons (10 mL) **kosher salt**
- 2 teaspoons (10 mL) **Kashmiri chili powder**
- 1 teaspoon (5 mL) minced **ginger**
- 3 tablespoons (45 mL) **jaggery** or **brown sugar**
- ¾ cup (175 mL) **apple cider vinegar**
- 2 cups (500 mL) small **cauliflower florets**
- 1 **serrano chile** or **green Thai chile**, thinly sliced
- 6 **carrots**, cut into short, thin strips

1   Using the Sauté function on High, heat the oil in the inner pot for about 1 minute, until shimmering. Add the smashed garlic cloves and cook, stirring occasionally, for about 3 minutes, until they start to brown and sputter. Stir in the mustard seeds, salt, chili powder and ginger; cook for about 1 minute, until the mustard seeds begin to pop. Add the jaggery and vinegar; cook for about 2 minutes, stirring occasionally, until the jaggery has dissolved.

2   Stir in the cauliflower, chile and carrots. Secure the lid and cook on low pressure for 5 minutes (you can also cook on high pressure for 2 minutes).

3   Once the cooking is complete, quick-release the pressure.

4   Remove the lid and stir. Serve immediately or let cool and store in an airtight container in the refrigerator for up to 1 month.

SPICY SOUTH INDIAN LIME PICKLE

VEG · GF · V

This pickle was always on the table at my grandparents' house when I was growing up, but I was deeply afraid of its tart lime flavor and all those ground chiles. These days I love adding it to Bengali Cholar Dal (page 195) or any rice or grain bowl with a fried egg—it adds a ton of oomph. This recipe calls for a tiny amount of asafoetida, which adds a lovely funkiness to anything it touches and pushes the salt, spice and tang to the nth degree. It's worth seeking out, but don't worry if you can't find it; the pickle still has loads of flavor without it.

- 10 **limes**, cut into eighths
- 1 tablespoon (15 mL) **kosher salt**
- 1 cup (250 mL) **water**
- 3 tablespoons (45 mL) **vegetable oil**
- 1 teaspoon (5 mL) **yellow mustard seeds**
- ¼ teaspoon (1 mL) **asafoetida**
- 1 teaspoon (5 mL) ground **turmeric**
- 1 teaspoon (5 mL) **fenugreek seeds**, ground
- 10 **dried red chiles**, toasted and coarsely ground (see page 20)

1 Place the limes, salt and water in the inner pot. Secure the lid and cook on high pressure for 6 minutes.

2 Once the cooking is complete, quick-release the pressure.

3 Using a slotted spoon, remove the limes from the inner pot and discard the water. Let cool slightly and then chop into ½-inch (1 cm) pieces.

4 Wipe the inner pot clean. Using the Sauté function on High, heat the oil for about 1 minute, until shimmering. Add the mustard seeds and cook for about 30 seconds, until they begin to pop. Stir in the asafoetida (if using), turmeric, ground fenugreek and chiles; cook for about 30 seconds, until fragrant. Add the limes and cook, stirring, for about 2 minutes, until fragrant and completely coated in the spice mixture.

5 Serve immediately or let cool and store in an airtight container in the refrigerator for up to 1 month.

CLEMENTINE GINGER Chutney

VEG **GF** **V**

With an Indian father and an Irish mother, I grew up with dozens of jars of chutneys and marmalades in our kitchen. This is a lovechild of the two, with wintery flavors from the orange and ginger, a hint of heat from the chile and a slightly bittersweet tang that resembles traditional marmalade. I like it served with roast pork (you can even use it as a glaze), smeared atop uttapams (page 249) or stirred into Tea-Braised Lamb Stew (page 222).

1½ pounds (750 g) **clementines**, finely chopped (including the rind)

1 tablespoon (15 mL) **kosher salt**

1 tablespoon (15 mL) **vegetable oil**

2 tablespoons (30 mL) minced **ginger**

1 teaspoon (5 mL) **cumin seeds**

6 **curry leaves**, torn into small pieces

6 fresh or frozen **makrut lime leaves**, center rib removed, torn into small pieces (see page 30)

1 **serrano chile**, minced

¼ cup (60 mL) **jaggery** or **brown sugar**

2 tablespoons (30 mL) **water**

2 tablespoons (30 mL) **red wine vinegar**

1 Place the clementines and salt in a large bowl and toss until evenly coated. Cover and refrigerate for at least 2 hours or up to 8 hours.

2 Using the Sauté function on High, heat the oil in the inner pot for about 1 minute, until shimmering. Add the ginger, cumin seeds, curry leaves and lime leaves; cook for 1 minute, until the cumin seeds are brown and fragrant. Add the chile, clementines with accumulated liquid, jaggery, water and vinegar; stir to combine, breaking up any chunks of jaggery with a spoon.

3 Secure the lid and cook on high pressure for 4 minutes.

4 Once the cooking is complete, let the pressure release naturally for 5 minutes, then quick-release the remaining pressure.

5 Remove the lid. Using the Sauté function on High, cook the chutney for about 3 minutes, stirring often, until the juices thicken to a syrupy consistency. Serve immediately or let cool and store in an airtight container in the refrigerator for up to 1 month.

CHERRY TOMATO (VEG) (GF) (V)
CHUTNEY

Traditional Indian tomato chutney is a smooth purée, but I prefer mine chunkier, more like a salsa. If you can't find fresh curry leaves, basil is an acceptable substitute here; the flavor will have more of an herbaceous Italian vibe but it will still be pretty tasty. You can serve this chutney alongside vegetables, rice, meat or fish, or spoon it atop fresh naan with a little soft paneer for an Indian take on bruschetta.

- 1 tablespoon (15 mL) **vegetable oil**
- 2 teaspoons (10 mL) **mustard seeds**
- 1 teaspoon (5 mL) **cumin seeds**
- 1 teaspoon (5 mL) **nigella seeds**
- 10 fresh **curry leaves** or **basil leaves**, torn into pieces
- 1 teaspoon (5 mL) ground **turmeric**
- 4 cups (1 L) **cherry tomatoes**
- 1 teaspoon (5 mL) **kosher salt**
- 1 tablespoon (15mL) **jaggery** or **brown sugar**

1 Using the Sauté function on High, heat the oil in the inner pot for about 1 minute, until shimmering. Add the mustard seeds, cumin seeds, nigella seeds and curry leaves; cook for about 2 minutes, stirring occasionally, until the leaves are just beginning to crackle and the seeds begin to pop. Add the turmeric and tomatoes; stir to combine. Add the salt and jaggery; stir to combine.

2 Secure the lid and cook on low pressure for 5 minutes (you can also cook it on high pressure for 3 minutes).

3 Once the cooking is complete, quick-release the pressure.

4 Remove the lid. Using the Sauté function on High, cook for about 2 or 3 minutes, stirring occasionally and gently mashing half of the tomatoes with the back of a spoon, until the liquid has reduced by about half. Serve warm or at room temperature, or let cool and store in an airtight container in the refrigerator for up to 3 days.

NOTE *The liquid the tomatoes release has loads of flavor. Sometimes I drain it off instead of cooking it down, so that I can blend it with any leftover tomato chutney to make a spiced tomato soup.*

(VEG) (GF) (V)

MANGO CHUTNEY

If you've eaten any chutney in your lifetime, it's probably been mango. Usually mango chutney is really sweet, to the point of being cloying. Since I like eating it with pork and chicken, I prefer my chutney a little more on the tart side. Make sure your mangoes are just barely ripe, so they hold their shape and don't turn into a complete mush after cooking.

- 1 tablespoon (15 mL) **vegetable oil**
- 1 teaspoon (5 mL) **yellow mustard seeds**
- ½ teaspoon (2 mL) **coriander seeds**
- 3 **green cardamom pods**, smashed
- ½ small **white onion**, minced
- 2 firm, ripe **mangoes**, peeled and chopped
- 1 **dried red chile**, broken into pieces
- ¼ cup (60 mL) **apple cider vinegar**
- 2 tablespoons (30 mL) **jaggery** or **brown sugar**

1 Using the Sauté function on High, heat the oil in the inner pot for about 1 minute, until shimmering. Add the mustard seeds, coriander seeds, smashed cardamom pods and onion; cook, stirring frequently, for about 4 minutes, until the onion has softened.

2 Add the mangoes, chile and vinegar; stir to combine. Secure the lid and cook on high pressure for 6 minutes.

3 Once the cooking is complete, let the pressure release naturally for 5 minutes, then quick-release the remaining pressure.

4 Remove the lid and stir in the jaggery. Using the Sauté function on Normal, cook, stirring often and breaking up the pieces of jaggery, for about 4 minutes, until the liquid has reduced to a syrupy consistency. Serve immediately or let cool and store in an airtight container in the refrigerator for up to 2 weeks.

CRANBERRY CHUTNEY

VEG · GF · V

This chutney is tasty year-round, but it will shine at Thanksgiving dinner—I promise you, it is one of the few cranberry chutneys that are actually eaten during the meal. The rest of the year it's delicious on a ham or turkey sandwich, served with Rogan Ghosh (page 219), or on a cheese platter.

Food processor or blender

- 2 teaspoons (10 mL) **vegetable oil**
- 1 small **onion**, minced
- ¼ cup (60 mL) minced **ginger**
- 3 tablespoons (45 mL) **jaggery** or **brown sugar**
- 1 teaspoon (5 mL) **yellow mustard seeds**
- ½ teaspoon (2 mL) ground **cinnamon**
- ½ teaspoon (2 mL) ground **cardamom**
- ½ teaspoon (2 mL) ground **cloves**
- ½ teaspoon (2 mL) freshly ground **black pepper**
- 1 teaspoon (5 mL) **kosher salt**
- 12 ounces (375 g) fresh or frozen **cranberries** (3 cups/750 mL)
- 1 **orange** (including rind), roughly chopped

1 Using the Sauté function on High, heat the oil in the inner pot for about 1 minute, until shimmering. Add the onion and ginger; cook, stirring occasionally, for 3 to 4 minutes, until the onion has softened somewhat. Add the jaggery, mustard seeds, cinnamon, cardamom, cloves, pepper and salt; cook, stirring occasionally, for about 2 minutes, until the spices are fragrant. Stir in the cranberries and orange.

2 Secure the lid and cook on high pressure for 5 minutes.

3 Once the cooking is complete, let the pressure release naturally.

4 Transfer the chutney to a food processor; pulse until evenly chopped but still chunky. Serve immediately or let cool completely and store in an airtight container in the refrigerator for up to 2 weeks.

PERSIMMON Chutney

VEG GF V

Persimmons are one of the best treats in winter, showing up just when you start feeling like you'll never see colorful produce again. This chutney is like sunshine during those dark months. Make sure you use Fuyu persimmons here; they look a bit like orange tomatoes with leafy tops. I like to eat it with a light cheese such as Soft Paneer (page 67) and crackers.

2 tablespoons (30 mL) **vegetable oil**

½ cup (125 mL) minced **onion**

1 teaspoon (5 mL) ground **cumin**

1 teaspoon (5 mL) ground **coriander**

1 teaspoon (5 mL) **kosher salt** (approx.)

1 teaspoon (5 mL) **yellow mustard seeds**

1 tablespoon (15 mL) minced **ginger**

4 **Fuyu persimmons**, peeled and chopped

2 tablespoons (30 mL) **apple cider vinegar**

1 Using the Sauté function on High, heat the oil in the inner pot for about 1 minute, until shimmering. Add the onion and cook, stirring occasionally, for about 4 minutes, until softened. Add the cumin, coriander, salt and mustard seeds; cook for about 1 minute, until the mustard seeds begin to pop.

2 Stir in the ginger and persimmons, then add the vinegar. Using a wooden spoon, stir, scraping up any browned bits on the bottom of the pot.

3 Secure the lid and cook on high pressure for 3 minutes.

4 Once the cooking is complete, let the pressure release naturally for 5 minutes, then quick-release the remaining pressure.

5 Remove the lid and stir the chutney. If it is too thin for your liking, simmer, using the Sauté function on High, stirring frequently, until it thickens to your taste. Season to taste with salt. Serve immediately or let cool to room temperature and store in an airtight container in the refrigerator for up to 2 weeks.

PREP
5 MIN

TOTAL
6 MIN
(PLUS 20 MIN
TO SOAK)

MAKES
2 CUPS
(500 ML)

COCONUT CILANTRO CHUTNEY

VEG **GF**

The day my sister-in-law, Ketan, first made me this chutney was one of the great food days of my life—it's incredible. I serve it as a dip with papadums and Naan (page 252), spread over Coconut Cilantro Steamed Fish (page 225) or—my favorite—smeared onto Aloo Tikki Pav (page 117).

Food processor or blender

2   cups (500 mL) unsweetened **coconut flakes**

1   cup (250 mL) **milk** (see Note)

1   **serrano chile**, minced

2   cups (500 mL) roughly chopped **cilantro**

1   cup (250 mL) **mint** leaves

2   teaspoon (10 mL) minced **ginger**

2   teaspoons (10 mL) minced **garlic**

1   teaspoon (5 mL) **kosher salt**

1   teaspoon (5 mL) **cumin seeds**

¼   cup (60 mL) freshly squeezed **lime juice**

¼   cup (60 mL) **water**

1   Combine the coconut flakes and milk in a medium bowl; soak for 20 minutes. Drain.

2   Place the coconut, chiles, cilantro, mint, ginger, garlic, salt and cumin seeds in a food processor; process until thick and smooth.

3   Stop the motor and scrape down the sides of the bowl. Add the lime juice and water; process until smooth, adding more water if needed to create a smooth consistency. Serve immediately or store in an airtight container in the refrigerator for up to 1 week.

NOTE   *To make this recipe vegan, substitute full-fat coconut milk for the milk.*

SAFFRON VEG GF V
CITRUS TOMATO PEACH
CHUTNEY

This chutney/marmalade hybrid is the result of one of those kitchen disasters that wind up even better than what you originally intended. I got distracted (damn you, Internet) while the chutney was simmering, and it burned in the pot. I transferred it to another pot and, while praying that it wasn't ruined, inhaled and smelled toasted sugar and citrus goodness. The sugars were deeply caramelized and the flavor was much richer than I had expected. It was totally worth the giant burnt spot in the pot! Once I figured out how to make it—without burning my Instant Pot—it became one of my favorite sweet, tangy spreads.

8	ounces (250 g)	**lemons**
8	ounces (250 g)	**oranges**
1	cup (250 mL)	**water**
2	pounds (1 kg)	**Roma tomatoes**
3	**peaches** (see Note)	
2½	pounds (1.25 kg)	**jaggery** or **brown sugar**
¼	cup (60 mL) freshly squeezed **lemon juice**	
	Large pinch **saffron**	
1	teaspoon (5 mL) **Garam Masala** (page 24) or store-bought	

NOTE *If you can't find fresh peaches, use thawed frozen peaches instead. You could also just omit them.*

1 Cut the lemons and oranges in quarters lengthwise and remove the seeds. Cut each quarter crosswise into thin slices.

2 Place the lemon and orange slices in the inner pot. Pour the water over the fruit and cook on high pressure for 10 minutes.

3 Meanwhile, bring a medium saucepan of water to a boil. Add the tomatoes and peaches and cook for 1 minute, until the skins lighten in color and start to release from the tomatoes. Immediately transfer the tomatoes and peaches to a bowl of ice water. Once they are cool enough to handle, peel and tear the flesh into 1-inch (2.5 cm) pieces, discarding the skins of both and the seeds of the tomatoes.

4 Once the lemons and oranges are cooked, let the pressure release naturally.

5 Place a small plate and 3 or 4 metal teaspoons in your freezer (you'll need these for testing the chutney's consistency).

6 Remove the lid and stir in the jaggery. Add the tomatoes, peaches, lemon juice, saffron and garam masala; stir to combine. Using the Sauté function on High, bring the mixture to a boil. Cook at a rapid boil for about 30 minutes, stirring occasionally, until the mixture begins to foam. Once it is foaming, stir more frequently, making sure to scrape the bottom of the pot so the sugars don't stick and burn. You'll see fewer

bubbles as the chutney gets close to being done; continue to stir frequently. The chutney will be ready for testing when it is shiny and the bubbles are very small.

7   Turn off the Instant Pot. Remove the plate and one teaspoon from the freezer. Using the frozen teaspoon, spoon a small amount of chutney onto the frozen plate. Return the plate to the freezer for 3 to 4 minutes, then take it out and tilt it. The chutney shouldn't slide down the plate and the top layer should resemble jelly. If it's too thin and slides around on the plate, turn on the

Sauté function again and cook the chutney for another 3 minutes, stirring frequently. Then repeat the test.

8   Once the cooking is complete, turn off the heat but do not stir the chutney. Using a stainless steel spoon, skim off any surface foam and discard it. Pour the chutney into airtight containers and let cool, then refrigerate for up to 1 month or freeze for up to 1 year. (You can also pour the chutney into sterilized canning jars, seal the jars with two-piece lids and process according to your preferred canning method.)

SNACKS

and

CHAATS

SPICED CARROT
BHARTA

 (SPICY CARROT DIP)

I love all kinds of spreads and dips. They are lifesavers when it comes to entertaining, and just as nice to have around on regular days, as snacks, a light lunch or a sandwich spread. This carrot bharta perfectly fits the bill: it's easy to make and full of spices and bright flavors. Serve it with raw veggies, chips, fried papadums or pieces of Naan (page 252).

Food processor or blender

- 3 tablespoons (45 mL) **vegetable oil**
- 1 pound (500 g) **carrots**, cut crosswise into thirds
- 2 **garlic cloves**, roughly chopped
- 1 teaspoon (5 mL) ground **cumin**
- 1 teaspoon (5 mL) **smoked paprika**
- 1 teaspoon (5 mL) **Garam Masala** (page 24) or store-bought
- ½ teaspoon (2 mL) ground **coriander**
- 1 teaspoon (5 mL) **kosher salt** (approx.)
- ¾ cup (175 mL) dried **red lentils**, rinsed
- ¾ cup (175 mL) **water**

1 Using the Sauté function on High, heat the oil in the inner pot for about 1 minute, until shimmering. Add the carrots and cook, stirring occasionally, for about 5 minutes, until lightly browned. Stir in the garlic, cumin, paprika, garam masala, coriander and salt. Add the lentils and water; stir to combine.

2 Secure the lid and cook on high pressure for 10 minutes.

3 Once the cooking is complete, let the pressure release naturally for 5 minutes, then quick-release the remaining pressure.

4 Remove the lid and stir the mixture. Transfer to a food processor or blender. Let cool slightly, then pulse until thick and smooth. Taste and add more salt if needed. Serve immediately or let cool and store in an airtight container in the refrigerator for up to 3 days.

POTATO PEA (VEG)
SAMOSAS

The potato samosa is the little black dress of Indian snacks: timeless, popular and easy to dress up or down with dipping sauces, like Beet Raita (page 60) or Coriander Lemon Chutney (page 78). You can also use other ingredients for the filling; feel free to add some chopped spinach or any other greens you have sitting around. I keep a bag of prepped samosas in my freezer so I can pull them out at the first sign of samosa cravings or last-minute guests.

- 1 pound (500 g) **yellow-fleshed potatoes**, quartered
- 1 cup (250 mL) **water** (approx.)
- **Ghee**
- 1 **onion**, minced
- 1 tablespoon (15 mL) **Garam Masala** (page 24) or store-bought
- 1 teaspoon (5 mL) ground **cumin**
- 2 **green Thai chiles**, minced
- 4 **garlic cloves**, minced
- 2 teaspoons (10 mL) **kosher salt** (approx.)
- 2 cups (500 mL) frozen **peas**, thawed
- ½ cup (125 mL) minced **cilantro**
- 2 sheets (each 10 by 15 inches/25 by 38 cm) **puff pastry dough**, thawed if frozen
- 1 tablespoon (15 mL) **Chaat Masala** (page 25) or store-bought

1 Place the potatoes in the inner pot and pour the water overtop. Secure the lid and cook on low pressure for 12 minutes (you can also cook on high pressure for 8 minutes).

2 Once the cooking is complete, quick-release the pressure.

3 Using a slotted spoon, transfer the potatoes to a bowl. Reserve about ¼ cup (60 mL) cooking liquid; discard the excess. Let the potatoes cool slightly, then remove and discard the skins. Wipe the inner pot clean.

4 Using the Sauté function on High, heat 3 tablespoons (45 mL) ghee in the inner pot for 1 minute, until shimmering. Add the onion, garam masala and cumin; cook, stirring occasionally, for about 4 minutes, until the onions have softened. Add the chiles, garlic and salt; cook, stirring, for about 1 minute, until fragrant.

5 Turn off the machine and return the potatoes to the inner pot. Mash with a potato masher, adding the reserved cooking water if needed to attain a smooth and creamy consistency. Taste and add more salt if needed. Fold in the peas and cilantro.

6 Preheat the oven to 400°F (200°C).

7 Place one sheet of puff pastry on a work surface and roll out into a 15-inch (38 cm) square. Cut the pastry into 12 smaller squares. Brush the edges of each square with water, then spoon 3 tablespoons (45 mL) potato filling onto one corner, ¼ inch (0.5 cm) from the moistened edge. Fold the corner over the filling to form a triangle, pressing down on the edges to seal. Place on a baking sheet. Repeat with the remaining squares of puff pastry and filling until you have 24 samosas, spacing at least 1 inch (2.5 cm) apart.

8 Bake in the preheated oven for about 20 minutes, until browned and crispy. Remove the samosas from the oven, sprinkle with chaat masala and serve with your favorite chutney.

NOTES *You can make the samosas in advance through the end of Step 7, then freeze in an airtight container for up to 2 months. Bake from frozen, adding 5 minutes to the baking time.*

Any leftover samosas can be reheated in a 400°F (200°C) oven for 5 minutes.

LAMB VINDALOO
SAMOSAS

Vindaloo was created by the Portuguese, who ruled Goa, on the southeastern coast of India, for 400 years; *vindaloo* is Portuguese for meat in a garlic and wine marinade. Here it's a filling for samosas. My friend Cory Morris, a chef in Chicago, taught me to use a stand mixer to shred braised meat quickly. It's a big help if you are the person in a rush scrambling to shred meat that is still hot (ummm … me). If you don't have a mixer, just let the meat cool down a bit and shred it with your hands or two forks. You can double this recipe to make a large pot of vindaloo for dinner (or a million samosas).

Coffee/spice grinder
Stand mixer (optional)

- 1 tablespoon (15 mL) **cumin seeds**
- 1 tablespoon (15 mL) **coriander seeds**
- 1 tablespoon (15 mL) **kosher salt** (approx.)
- 1 teaspoon (5 mL) **black peppercorns**
- 6 whole **cloves**
- ½ teaspoon (2 mL) **cardamom seeds**
- 2 **dried red chiles**, torn into pieces
- 1 pound (500 g) boneless **lamb shoulder**, trimmed and cubed
- 2 tablespoons (30 mL) **vegetable oil**
- 1 **onion**, chopped
- 1 tablespoon (15 mL) minced **ginger**
- 5 **garlic cloves**, minced
- ¼ cup (60 mL) **red wine vinegar**
- ¼ cup (60 mL) **water**
- 12 sheets (each 15 by 10 inches/38 by 25 cm) **phyllo pastry**, thawed if frozen (1 lb/500 g)

1 Combine the cumin seeds, coriander seeds, salt, peppercorns, cloves, cardamom seeds and chiles in a clean coffee/spice grinder; grind to a powder.

2 Combine the lamb and the spice mixture in a large bowl. Cover and refrigerate for at least 1 hour or up to 12 hours.

3 Using the Sauté function on High, heat the oil in the inner pot for 1 minute, until shimmering. Add the onion; cook, stirring frequently, for about 4 minutes, until softened. Add the seasoned lamb and cook, stirring often, for about 5 minutes, until browned. Stir in the ginger and garlic; cook for about 1 minute, until fragrant.

4 Add the red wine vinegar and water. Using a wooden spoon, stir, scraping up any browned bits on the bottom of the pot. Secure the lid and cook on high pressure for 20 minutes.

5 Once the cooking is complete, let the pressure release naturally for 10 minutes, then quick-release the remaining pressure.

6 Transfer the lamb and cooking liquid to the bowl of a stand mixer and let cool slightly. Using the paddle attachment, process the lamb until shredded. Let cool completely. (If you don't have a stand mixer, let the meat cool slightly, then shred using your hands or two forks.)

7 Preheat oven to 375°F (190°C).

8 Unroll the phyllo pastry onto the countertop and cover with a piece of plastic wrap topped with a dampened clean tea towel. Place one sheet of phyllo on a clean work surface and brush with ghee. Working quickly, so the pastry doesn't dry out, top it with another sheet of phyllo; then cut the layered phyllo into 4 lengthwise strips.

9 Spoon 2 tablespoons (30 mL) lamb filling onto one corner of a phyllo strip. Fold the pastry over the filling to form a triangle. Keep folding the phyllo like a flag, enclosing the filling and forming a triangle. Place the samosa on a baking sheet with the seam side down. Repeat with the remaining phyllo pastry and filling until you have 24 samosas, spacing them at least ½ inch (2 cm) apart. Brush the tops of the samosas with ghee.

10 Bake in the preheated oven for about 25 minutes, until browned and crispy. Serve with your favorite chutney.

NOTES *I like serving these with fruit chutney such as Persimmon Chutney (page 91) or Coconut Cilantro Chutney (page 92), which balances the spiced meat.*

You can make these in advance through the end of Step 8 and then freeze in an airtight container for up to 2 months. Bake from frozen, adding 5 minutes to the baking time.

BAINGAN BHARTA

VEG · **GF** · **V** (SMOKY EGGPLANT DIP)

There are a lot of similarities among the cuisines of countries along the old spice routes, and you can taste that in this eggplant dip, which is reminiscent of baba ghanoush, but with a distinctly Indian point of view. Serve it with fried papadums, raw veggies, tortilla chips, roti or Naan (page 252).

Food processor or blender

- 1 pound (500 g) **eggplant**
- 1 tablespoon (15 mL) **vegetable oil**, divided
- 1 **onion**, finely chopped
- 2 teaspoons (10 mL) ground **cumin**
- 1 teaspoon (5 mL) ground **turmeric**
- 1 teaspoon (5 mL) **Garam Masala** (page 24) or store-bought
- 1 teaspoon (5 mL) **smoked paprika**
- 2 teaspoons (10 mL) minced **ginger**
- 4 **garlic cloves**, minced
- ½ cup (125 mL) **water**
- 2 **tomatoes**, chopped
- 1 teaspoon (5 mL) **kosher salt** (approx.)
- ½ tsp (2 mL) freshly ground **black pepper**
- ¼ cup (60 mL) minced fresh **cilantro**

NOTE *If you have access to a grill, you can use it to char the eggplant. If not, placing it over a gas burner will create enough smoky flavor to make this spread special.*

1 Rub the eggplant with ½ teaspoon (2 mL) of the oil.

2 Place the eggplant directly over a gas burner set to high heat and roast, turning occasionally, for about 10 minutes, until tender and charred on all sides. If you do not have a gas stove (see Note), rub the eggplant with oil, halve it lengthwise and place it cut side down on a rimmed baking sheet. Preheat your oven to 450°F (230°C) and bake for about 45 minutes, until tender and charred on all sides.

3 Let the eggplant cool to room temperature. Peel off and discard the charred skin and roughly chop the flesh.

4 Using the Sauté function on High, heat the remaining oil in the inner pot for about 1 minute, until shimmering. Add the onion; cook, stirring occasionally, for about 4 minutes, until softened. Stir in the cumin, turmeric, garam masala, paprika, ginger and garlic; cook for about 1 minute, until fragrant. Add the water and, using a wooden spoon, stir, scraping up any browned bits on the bottom of the pot. Stir in the tomatoes, eggplant with accumulated juices, salt and pepper.

5 Secure the lid and cook on high pressure for 5 minutes.

6 Once the cooking is complete, let the pressure release naturally for 5 minutes, then quick-release the remaining pressure.

7 Remove the lid and transfer the mixture to a food processor. Let cool slightly, then pulse until thick and smooth. Add more salt if needed. Serve immediately or let cool completely and store in an airtight container in the refrigerator for up to 3 days. Served topped with cilantro.

Idli CHAAT

GF VEG (FRIED LENTIL AND RICE CAKES)

Creating new uses for leftovers makes me immeasurably happy, especially when the result is a crispy, tangy, spicy plateful of fried idli. These fermented lentil and rice cakes are most often served at breakfast or lunch in South India, but once they have been fried and spiced up, they are ready for the cocktail hour.

¼ cup (60 mL) **vegetable oil** or **ghee**, divided

6 cooked **Idlis** (page 237) or store-bought, cut into eighths

1 **red onion**, finely chopped

1 **bell pepper**, thinly sliced

2 **garlic cloves**, minced

2 teaspoons (10 mL) **Kashmiri chili powder**

4 fresh **curry leaves**, torn into pieces (optional)

½ cup (125 mL) **Plain Yogurt** (page 40) or store-bought

1 teaspoon (5 mL) **cumin seeds**, toasted (page 20)

2 teaspoons (10 mL) freshly squeezed **lemon juice**

¼ cup (60 mL) chopped fresh **cilantro**

¼ cup (60 mL) **peanuts** or **cashews**, toasted (page 32)

1   Using the Sauté function on High, heat 2 tablespoons (30 mL) oil in the inner pot for about 1 minute, until shimmering. Add the idli and cook, stirring occasionally, for about 2 minutes, until starting to crisp around the edges. Transfer the idli to a small bowl.

2   Add the remaining 2 tablespoons (30 mL) oil, onion and bell pepper to the inner pot; cook, stirring occasionally, for about 4 minutes, until softened. Stir in the garlic, chili powder and curry leaves; cook for about 1 minute, until fragrant. Return the fried idli to the inner pot and toss to coat with the onion mixture.

3   Place the yogurt in a shallow medium bowl. Add the cumin seeds and lemon juice; stir to combine. Spoon the fried idli and onion mixture over the yogurt, then top with the cilantro and peanuts; serve.

PREP
5 MIN

TOTAL
1 HR 15 MIN
(PLUS 1 HR 20
MIN TO MAKE
THE SAMOSAS)

SERVES
6

SAMOSA CHAAT SALAD

This is a great way to make yourself feel better about eating samosas or to use up leftover ones (but why do you have uneaten samosas???). Here the samosas are chopped up, dressed with chutney and served in a tangle of salad greens—it's my idea of a beautiful mess. This recipe comes together in just a few minutes if you have prepped samosas in the freezer.

12 **Potato Pea Samosas** (page 100) or **Lamb Vindaloo Samosas** (page 104)

½ cup (125 mL) **tamarind concentrate**

8 ounces (250 g) **arugula** or **mixed salad greens**

¼ cup (60 mL) **Coconut Cilantro Chutney** (page 92) or store-bought

1 cup (250 mL) **pomegranate seeds**

1 Place the samosas on a cutting board and cut into thirds.

2 Combine the samosa pieces and tamarind chutney in a large bowl; toss to coat. Place the arugula on a serving platter.

3 Transfer the samosas to the serving platter, arranging on top of the arugula. Spoon the cilantro chutney overtop, sprinkle with pomegranate seeds and serve.

CHICKPEA Chaat

VEG **GF** (CHILLED CHICKPEA SALAD)

My friends Zeeshan Shah and Yoshi Yamada of Chicago's Bombay Breakdown create some of my favorite takes on Indian street food and snacks. I can't resist this chaat when it's on the menu, so I recreated my own version at home, adding toasted cashews and pomegranate seeds. This is the kind of food I'll snack on all day.

- 1 cup (250 mL) dried **chickpeas**, picked over and rinsed (see page 29), about 8 ounces (250 g)
- 2 teaspoons (10 mL) **kosher salt**, divided
  Water
- 4 teaspoons (20 mL) **Chaat Masala** (page 25) or store-bought, divided
- 1 **English cucumber**, diced
- 1 cup (250 mL) **pomegranate seeds**
- 1 cup (250 mL) roughly chopped fresh **cilantro** leaves
- ½ cup (125 mL) roughly chopped fresh **mint** leaves
- 1 bunch **green onions**, sliced and divided
- 6 tablespoons (90 mL) freshly squeezed **lime juice**, divided
- 1 cup (250 mL) **Plain Yogurt** (page 40) or store-bought
- 1 **serrano chile**, minced
- ½ cup (125 mL) roasted **cashews** (page 32)
- ½ cup (125 mL) **fried bhel chips** or **crushed tortilla chips**
- ½ cup (125 mL) **fried chana dal** or **crushed tortilla chips**
- ½ cup (125 mL) **sev** or **crisp rice cereal**

1 Place the chickpeas and 1 teaspoon (5 mL) salt in the inner pot. Add enough water to cover by 3 inches (7.5 cm).

2 Secure the lid and cook on high pressure for 35 minutes.

3 Once the cooking is complete, let the pressure release naturally. Check to make sure the chickpeas are soft enough for your liking (if they are still too hard, cook on high pressure for another 5 minutes). Drain.

4 Combine the cooked chickpeas with 2 teaspoons (10 mL) chaat masala in a large bowl. Add the cucumber, pomegranate seeds, cilantro, mint and half of the green onions. Toss the mixture with 4 tablespoons (60 mL) lime juice.

5 Place the yogurt in a medium bowl and stir in the remaining 2 tablespoons (30 mL) lime juice, 1 teaspoon (5 mL) salt and green onions, plus the chile.

6 Spoon the yogurt mixture over the chickpea mixture. Top with cashews, bhel chips, chana dal and sev. Sprinkle the remaining 2 teaspoons (10 mL) chaat masala overtop; serve immediately.

NOTE *You can prepare this recipe in advance through to the end of Step 5, but make sure not to add the crunchy components until just before serving. If you want to get fancy for a cocktail party, spoon this chaat into Belgian endive spears, which will double as edible scoops.*

VEG GF FRIED CHILI PANEER

Yes, it's fried cheese. It's also coated in a sweet, spicy, sticky sauce. Is there anything else you need to know? I don't think so, except that you should make more of this than you think you need. A platter of these crispy, gooey bites goes fast.

- 2 teaspoons (10 mL) **Kashmiri chili powder**
- 1 teaspoon (5 mL) **Curry Powder** (page 23) or store-bought
- ½ teaspoon (2 mL) **kosher salt**
- ¼ cup (60 mL) **vegetable oil**, divided
- 14 ounces (420 g) **Firm Paneer** (page 68) or store-bought, cubed
- 2 teaspoons (10 mL) minced **ginger**
- 2 **garlic cloves**, minced
- 2 **green onions**, minced
- 2 teaspoons (10 mL) **tamari** or **soy sauce**
- ½ cup (125 mL) **Thai sweet chili sauce**

1 Combine the chili powder, curry powder and salt in a large bowl. Add the paneer and toss to coat in the spice mixture.

2 Using the Sauté function on High, heat 2 tablespoons (30 mL) oil in the inner pot for about 90 seconds, until very hot. Add half the paneer; cook, turning occasionally, for about 4 minutes, until the cheese is browned on all sides. Transfer the cooked paneer to a plate lined with paper towels. Repeat with the remaining oil and paneer.

3 Add the ginger, garlic and green onions to the inner pot; cook, stirring occasionally, for about 90 seconds, until fragrant. Stir in the tamari and chili sauce.

4 Place the fried paneer in a shallow bowl or on a platter. Spoon the sauce overtop and serve.

NOTE *You can fry the paneer an hour or so before serving and keep warm in a 200°F (100°C) oven. Make sure to keep the sauce and paneer separate if you're making this ahead; it will get soggy if it's combined too early.*

GF .LAMB MEATBALLS

These meatballs make a lovely little party appetizer, especially when you serve them with Cucumber Raita (page 56), Persimmon Chutney (page 91), Coconut Cilantro Chutney (page 92) or even just some yogurt seasoned with cumin and lime juice. I love to eat any leftovers wrapped in a piece of chapatti, naan or pita, adding a generous schmear of raita. Make sure you mince the onion and herbs very finely so you don't end up with large chunks in the meatballs.

Instant Pot trivet

- 2   teaspoons (10 mL) ground **cumin**
- 1   teaspoon (5 mL) **kosher salt**
- 1   teaspoon (5 mL) freshly ground **black pepper**
- 1   teaspoon (5 mL) ground **cardamom**
- 1   tablespoon (15 mL) minced fresh **cilantro** leaves
- 1   tablespoon (15 mL) minced fresh **mint** leaves
- 4   **garlic cloves**, minced
- ½   small **red onion**, minced
- 1   pound (500 g) **ground lamb**
- 1   cup (250 mL) **water**
- 2   tablespoons (30 mL) **vegetable oil**

1   Using the Sauté function on Normal, cook the cumin, salt, pepper and cardamom in the inner pot for about 1 minute, until fragrant. Transfer the spices to a large bowl and shake until evenly combined. Add the cilantro and mint; toss to combine. Add the garlic and onion; toss to combine.

2   Add the lamb to the spice mixture; using your hands, gently combine until the ingredients are evenly distributed (don't overmix, or the meatballs will be tough).

3   Place the trivet in the inner pot and add the water. Place a small plate on top of the trivet.

4   Using a tablespoon (15 mL) or mini ice-cream scoop, scoop up the mixture and shape into 24 small meatballs. Place the meatballs on the plate in the inner pot, stacking if necessary.

5   Secure the lid and cook on high pressure for 5 minutes.

6   Once the cooking is complete, let the pressure release naturally for 5 minutes, then quick-release the remaining pressure. Remove the plate, trivet and meatballs. Empty the water and wipe out the pot.

7   Using the Sauté function on High, heat 1 tablespoon (15 mL) oil for about 1 minute, until shimmering. Sear half the meatballs in batches, turning frequently, for about 4 minutes, until browned on all sides and no longer pink inside. Use the remaining 1 tablespoon (15 mL) oil to cook the remaining meatballs.

8   Transfer the meatballs to a platter; serve with raita or chutney for dipping.

ALOO TIKKI PAV

 **(FRIED POTATO SLIDERS)**

The magic that is a fried mashed-potato cake smeared with herby chutney and sandwiched by a soft bun is reason enough to visit India—I don't know why it isn't in tourism ads with photos of the Taj Mahal. This is the type of snack you can buy at a roadside stall in Hyderabad or Mumbai and eat as you walk along. But at home, I serve these as vegetarian sliders for a barbecue. You can form the patties earlier in the day and keep them in the refrigerator until you're ready to cook.

- 1 pound (500 g) **yellow-fleshed potatoes**, quartered
- 1 cup (250 mL) **water**
- ⅓ cup (75 mL) **ghee** or **vegetable oil**, divided (approx.)
- 1 **onion**, minced
- 1 teaspoon (5 mL) ground **cumin**
- 1 teaspoon (5 mL) ground **turmeric**
- 2 small **green chiles**, minced
- 4 **garlic cloves**, minced
- 2 teaspoons (10 mL) **kosher salt** (approx.)
- ½ cup (125 mL) **all-purpose flour** (approx.)
- ½ cup (125 mL) chopped fresh **cilantro**
- 8 **slider buns**, split
- ¾ cup (175 mL) **Coconut Cilantro Chutney** (page 92) or store-bought

1 Place the potatoes in the inner pot and pour the water overtop. Secure the lid and cook on low pressure for 12 minutes (you can also cook on high pressure for 8 minutes).

2 Once the cooking is complete, quick-release the pressure.

3 Using a slotted spoon, transfer the potatoes to a bowl. Reserve about ¼ cup (60 mL) cooking liquid; discard the excess liquid and wipe the pot clean. Let the potatoes cool slightly, then remove and discard the skins.

4 Using the Sauté function on High, heat 3 tablespoons (45 mL) ghee in the inner pot for 1 minute, until shimmering. Add the onion, cumin and turmeric; cook, stirring occasionally, for about 4 minutes, until the onion has softened. Add the chiles, garlic and salt; cook, stirring, for about 1 minute, until fragrant.

5 Turn off the heat and return the potatoes to the inner pot. Mash with a potato masher until somewhat smooth, adding reserved potato-cooking water, if needed, so they are creamy. Taste the potatoes and add more salt if needed. Fold in the flour and cilantro.

6 Transfer the mashed potatoes to a lightly floured work surface. Divide into 8 equal portions and shape each into a patty 2 inches (5 cm) in diameter, adding more flour to the work surface if the potato is sticking.

7 Heat half of the remaining ghee in a large skillet. Add the potato patties, in batches if necessary, and cook for about 2 to 3 minutes per side, until crisp and browned, adding more ghee as necessary. Drain the patties on a plate lined with paper towels.

8 Place the patties in the slider buns, top with coconut chutney and eat, pretending you are at the side of a busy road in your own private heaven.

SWEET POTATO Pav Bhaji

VEG **V** (CURRIED VEGETABLE SLIDERS)

Pav bhajis are the vegetable sloppy joes of Indian street food, and I say that with a great deal of respect and affection. These feature sweet potatoes and are every bit as decadently messy as what you'll find on the streets of Mumbai. Make sure you toast the buns before topping them with the vegetables—you want that contrasting crunch when you bite into your pav.

- 2 tablespoons (30 mL) **vegetable oil** or **coconut oil**
- 1 **onion**, chopped
- 2 teaspoons (10 mL) **amchur powder** or **ground sumac**
- 1 teaspoon (5 mL) **Kashmiri chili powder**
- 2 teaspoons (10 mL) **kosher salt** (approx.)
- 2 teaspoons (10 mL) ground **coriander**
- 1 teaspoon (5 mL) **fennel seeds**
- 1 teaspoon (5 mL) ground **cumin**
- ¼ teaspoon (1 mL) ground **cloves**
- ½ teaspoon (2 mL) ground **cinnamon**
- ½ teaspoon (2 mL) ground **cardamom**
- ¼ teaspoon (1 mL) freshly ground **black pepper**
- 1 **serrano chile**, minced
- 4 **garlic cloves**, minced
- ½ cup (125 mL) **water**
- 1 can (14 oz/398 mL) diced **tomatoes** (with juice)
- 2 **sweet potatoes** (about 1¼ pounds/550 g), peeled and chopped into ¾-inch (2 cm) pieces (see Note)
- 12 **slider buns**, split and toasted

1 Using the Sauté function on High, heat the oil in the inner pot for 1 minute, until shimmering. Add the onion and stir to coat. Stir in the amchur, chili powder, salt, coriander, fennel seeds, cumin, cloves, cinnamon, cardamom, pepper, chile and garlic; cook for about 1 minute, until the spices are fragrant.

2 Stir in the water, using a wooden spoon to scrape up any browned bits on the bottom of the pot. Stir in the tomatoes (with juice) and add the sweet potatoes. Secure the lid and cook on high pressure for 5 minutes.

3 Once the cooking is complete, quick-release the pressure.

4 Remove the lid and stir to combine. Taste and add more salt if needed. Using the Sauté function on High, cook, stirring occasionally, for about 3 minutes, until the sauce has thickened slightly. Mash the sweet potatoes with a potato masher or wooden spoon, leaving some texture (you want this to have the consistency of a sloppy joe). Spoon the bhaji onto the slider buns and serve.

NOTE *Feel free to use butternut squash, pumpkin or any other winter squash instead of sweet potatoes in these sliders.*

SOUPS

Spiced VEG GF
BUTTERNUT SQUASH
SOUP

In winter, I turn into a soup-for-breakfast person, and this is exactly the kind of gently spiced, creamy, satisfying soup I love sipping all morning. (Hey, it's either that or eat doughnuts.) But don't get me wrong—the squash and warm spices make this soup rich enough to stand in for lunch or dinner, too. Don't skip the lime juice; it adds a brightness that makes this soup memorable.

Immersion blender or blender

- 3 tablespoons (45 mL) **ghee**, **coconut oil** or **vegetable oil**
- 1 medium **onion**, diced
- 2 **garlic cloves**, minced
- 1 tablespoon (15 mL) **kosher salt** (approx.)
- 2 teaspoons (10 mL) **Garam Masala** (page 24) or store-bought
- 1 teaspoon (5 mL) freshly ground **black pepper**
- 4 cups (1 L) low-sodium **vegetable broth**
- 2 pounds (1 kg) **butternut squash**, peeled, seeded and cut into large chunks
- 2 tablespoons (30 mL) freshly squeezed **lime juice** (approx.)
- 1 cup (250 mL) **heavy** or **whipping** (35%) **cream** (see Notes)

1 Using the Sauté function on High, heat the ghee in the inner pot for about 1 minute, until shimmering. Add the onion, garlic, salt, garam masala and pepper; cook, stirring occasionally, for about 4 minutes, until the onions have softened.

2 Add the vegetable broth; stir with a wooden spoon to scrape up any browned bits from the bottom of the pot. Add the butternut squash and secure the lid. Cook on high pressure for 10 minutes.

3 Once the cooking is complete, let the pressure release naturally for 10 minutes, then quick-release the remaining pressure. Remove the lid and turn off the Instant Pot. Let the soup cool slightly.

4 Purée the soup with an immersion blender or, working in batches, transfer to a blender and blend on high speed until smooth. Return the soup to the inner pot. Stir in 1 tablespoon (15 mL) lime juice; taste and add more if desired. Whisk in the cream. Taste and add additional salt, if needed; serve.

NOTES *Sometimes I substitute coconut milk (full-fat, always!) for the cream.*

Any hard winter squash will stand in for the butternut squash.

MULLIGA

A lot of people think mulligatawny is a traditional Indian soup, but it was actually created by the English living in Madras (now Chennai) back when India was a British colony. They added rice, more vegetables and sometimes meat to rasam, the traditional local soup, and christened the new version "mulligatawny," which is a Tamil word for "pepper water." Regardless of its origins, it has become part of Indian and European food culture. The no-fail combo of spices, apples and coconut makes it pretty hard to resist.

Blender or immersion blender

- 2 tablespoons (30 mL) **vegetable oil** or **coconut oil**
- 1 teaspoon (5 mL) **yellow mustard seeds**
- 2 **onions**, diced
- 1 tablespoon (15 mL) ground **cumin**
- 1 tablespoon (15 mL) ground **turmeric**
- 2 tablespoons (30 mL) **Curry Powder** (page 00) or store-bought
- 4 **garlic cloves**, minced
- 3 tablespoons (45 mL) minced **ginger**
- 1 tablespoon (15 mL) **kosher salt** (approx.)
- 2 teaspoons (10 mL) freshly ground **black pepper**
- 2 cups (500 mL) **water**
- ½ cup (125 mL) dried **red** or **yellow lentils**, rinsed

- 1 can (14 oz/398 mL) chopped **tomatoes** (with juice)
- 2 **Granny Smith apples**, peeled and chopped
- ½ cup (125 mL) white **basmati rice**, soaked and drained (see page 32)
- ½ cup (125 mL) chopped fresh **cilantro**, divided
- 1 can (14 oz/398 mL) full-fat **coconut milk**
- 2 tablespoons (30 mL) freshly squeezed **lime juice** (approx.)

TAWNY

  (CURRIED LENTIL, APPLE AND COCONUT MILK SOUP)

1   Using the Sauté function on High, heat the oil in the inner pot for about 1 minute, until shimmering. Add the mustard seeds; cook for about 1 minute, until the seeds begin to pop. Add the onions, cumin, turmeric and curry powder; stir to coat the onions in the spices and cook, stirring occasionally, for about 4 minutes, until the onions have softened. Stir in the garlic, ginger, salt and pepper; cook for about 1 minute, until fragrant.

2   Add the water. Using a wooden spoon, stir, scraping up any browned bits on the bottom of the pot. Stir in the lentils, tomatoes (with juice), apples, rice and ¼ cup (60 mL) cilantro.

3   Secure the lid and cook, using the Soup function on Normal, for 14 minutes.

4   Once the cooking is complete, let the pressure release naturally for 10 minutes, then quick-release the remaining pressure. Let cool slightly.

5   Remove the lid and stir in the coconut milk and lime juice. Working in batches, transfer three-quarters of the soup to a blender; blend at high speed until smooth. (You can also use an immersion blender to purée the soup, but make sure to leave a slightly chunky texture.) Pour the puréed mixture back into the inner pot and stir to combine. Season to taste with additional salt and lime juice, if needed. Garnish with the remaining cilantro and serve.

NOTES   *There are dozens of variations of mulligatawny, many including meat. If you want to add meat, stir in about 2 cups (500 mL) shredded cooked chicken after blending, for a heartier dish.*

   I sometimes add a dollop of yogurt as a garnish to make this soup even creamier (is anything ever creamy enough?).

CARROT GINGER
SOUP

VEG · **GF** · **V**

I have been making some version of this soup my whole life, depending on what I have in my kitchen. This is the kind of soup that welcomes change, whether it's a few parsnips or turnips mixed in with the carrots, a spoonful of curry powder, a little extra ginger or some lemongrass, if you have some on hand. The only rule is don't skimp on the coconut milk: full-fat milk gives this soup the creaminess that makes it so very good.

Immersion blender or blender

3 tablespoons (45 mL) **coconut oil** or **vegetable oil**

1 **onion**, diced

1 teaspoon (5 mL) ground **cumin**

1 teaspoon (5 mL) ground **turmeric**

1 teaspoon (5 mL) ground **coriander**

½ teaspoon (2 mL) **Kashmiri chili powder**

1 tablespoon (15 mL) minced **ginger**

1 pound (500 g) **carrots**, chopped

1 teaspoon (5 mL) **kosher salt** (approx.)

2 cups (500 mL) **water**

1 can (14 oz/398 mL) full-fat **coconut milk**

½ cup (125 mL) fresh **cilantro** leaves

1 Using the Sauté function on High, heat the oil in the inner pot for about 1 minute, until shimmering. Add the onion; cook, stirring occasionally, for about 4 minutes, until softened.

2 Add the cumin, turmeric, coriander and chili powder; stir to coat the onions in the spices. Add the ginger and cook, stirring, for 1 minute. Add the carrots, salt and water; stir to combine.

3 Secure the lid and cook on high pressure for 10 minutes.

4 Once the cooking is complete, let the pressure release naturally for 5 minutes, then quick-release the remaining pressure.

5 Remove the lid and let the soup cool slightly. Purée the soup with an immersion blender or, working in batches, transfer to a blender and blend on high speed until smooth. Return the soup to the inner pot and stir in the coconut milk. Taste and add more salt, if needed. Garnish with cilantro; serve.

ALOO GOBI
CHOWDER

VEG (CREAMY POTATO AND CAULIFLOWER SOUP)

This recipe emerged from a stream-of-consciousness moment while I was thinking about what to eat next (which I do a lot) and reading about replacing potatoes with cauliflower (which I would never do, such is my love for the spud). I thought about how much I love cauliflower and potatoes in aloo gobi, and then, recalling the year I spent cooking at a hotel in Maine making gallons of chowder every day, decided to turn aloo gobi into a chowder. The vadouvan spice blend used here is worth seeking out—it really makes the cauliflower sing.

2 tablespoons (30 mL) **ghee** or **vegetable oil**

2 **onions**, chopped into ½-inch (1 cm) pieces

2 tablespoons (30 mL) **vadouvan spice blend** or **curry powder** (see Note)

2 teaspoons (10 mL) ground **cumin**

4 **garlic cloves**, minced

1 tablespoon (15 mL) **kosher salt** (approx.)

¼ cup (60 mL) **all-purpose flour**

3 cups (750 mL) low-sodium **vegetable broth** or **water**

1 **cauliflower** head (about 1 pound/500 g), chopped into 1-inch (2.5 cm) pieces

1 pound (500 g) **yellow-fleshed, white-** or **red-skinned potatoes**, cut into ½-inch (1 cm) pieces

½ cup (125 mL) **heavy** or **whipping (35%) cream**

1 Using the Sauté function on High, heat the ghee in the inner pot for about 1 minute, until shimmering. Add the onions and cook, stirring occasionally, for about 4 minutes, until softened. Stir in the vadouvan, cumin, garlic and salt; cook for about 1 minute, until fragrant. Add the flour; stir to evenly coat the onions. Add the broth; stir, using a wooden spoon to scrape up any browned bits from the bottom of the pot. Stir in the cauliflower and potatoes.

2 Secure the lid and cook on high pressure for 7 minutes.

3 Once the cooking is complete, let the pressure release naturally for 10 minutes, then quick-release the remaining pressure.

4 Remove the lid and stir in the cream. Using the Sauté function on High, simmer for about 2 minutes, until the soup is thick and creamy. Season to taste with additional salt, if needed. Serve.

NOTES *Vadouvan is a French-created Indian spice blend that dates back to when France colonized Pondicherry. If you can't find it, use curry powder, which is a British-created Indian blend that uses some of the same spices.*

My friend Jen made this soup gluten-free by omitting the flour and puréeing about 1 cup (250 mL) of the cooked vegetables, then stirring it back into the soup; it gives you a thick, creamy texture without flour.

TOMATO ORANGE SAFFRON

VEG **GF** **V**

My brother Colin and I have a very specific memory of one night when we were kids, visiting our Uncle Madhav and Auntie Sarojani and their family in Kanpur, in northern India. We had just arrived on the train and were jet-lagged and exhausted by the unfamiliarity of everything. My auntie must have anticipated that her American niece and nephews would need a little familiarity, so she sat us down for bowls of tomato soup and cheese toast. At that moment I could have cried with relief, and decades later the memory still makes me smile. I think she made a fairly straightforward tomato soup, but I'm a nut for the combination of tomatoes, saffron and orange, so I added them to this version to remember that night with extra sunny warmth.

Blender or immersion blender

2   pounds (1 kg) **tomatoes**

3   tablespoons (45 mL) **coconut oil** or **vegetable oil**

3   **onions**, chopped

4   **carrots**, thinly sliced

6   large **garlic cloves**, minced

2   tablespoons (30 mL) grated **orange zest**

¼   teaspoon (1 mL) **Kashmiri chili powder**

½   teaspoon (2 mL) **fennel seeds**

1   **bay leaf**

¼   cup (60 mL) **tomato paste**

5   cups (1.25 L) **water**

1   cup (250 mL) **orange juice**

1   teaspoon (5 mL) **kosher salt** (approx.)
    Large pinch **saffron**

1   Bring a medium saucepan of water to a boil. Add the tomatoes and cook for 1 minute, until the skins lighten in color and start to release. Immediately transfer to a bowl of ice water. Once cool enough to handle, peel and tear the flesh into 1-inch (2.5 cm) pieces, discarding the skins and seeds. Set aside.

2   Using the Sauté function on Normal, heat the oil in the inner pot for about 1 minute, until shimmering. Add the onions, carrots, garlic, orange zest, chili powder, fennel seeds and bay leaf; cook, stirring occasionally, for about 10 minutes, until the vegetables are very soft but not brown.

3   Add the tomatoes and any accumulated juices, tomato paste, water, orange juice, salt and saffron. Secure the lid and cook, using the Soup function on Normal, for 10 minutes.

4   Once the cooking is complete, let the pressure release naturally.

5   Remove the lid and discard the bay leaf. Let cool slightly. Working in batches, transfer the soup to a blender and blend at high speed until smooth. (You can also use an immersion blender to purée the soup in the inner pot.) Taste and add more salt, if needed. Serve with cheesy toast if you want to give someone a hug.

NOTE *If fresh tomatoes aren't in season, use 1 can (28 oz/796 mL) whole tomatoes, with their juices. You might want to add 1 teaspoon (5 mL) granulated sugar if the canned tomatoes are too acidic.*

SPICED LENTIL SOUP.. VEG GF V

This recipe is essentially a dal (lentil stew) in soup form. It is one of my favorite things to make when I feel I need to be a little healthier—all that spinach reminds me of watching Popeye on TV when I was a kid. Eating this soup is like getting absolution after a night of eating too much junk food.

2 tablespoons (30 mL) **vegetable oil**

1 large **onion**, chopped

1 teaspoon (5 mL) **mustard seeds**

1 teaspoon (5 mL) **cumin seeds**

1 teaspoon (5 mL) ground **turmeric**

Pinch ground **fenugreek**

15 fresh **curry leaves**, torn into pieces

2 large **garlic cloves**, minced

1 **green Thai chile**, chopped

1 teaspoon (5 mL) **kosher salt**

½ teaspoon (2 mL) freshly ground **black pepper**

3 **carrots**, halved lengthwise and sliced

1 cup (250 mL) dried **green lentils**, rinsed

3 cups (750 mL) chopped **spinach** (see Note)

4 cups (1 L) low-sodium **vegetable broth**

½ cup (125 mL) chopped **cilantro**

1 Using the Sauté function on High, heat the oil in the inner pot for about 1 minute, until shimmering. Add the onion; cook, stirring occasionally, for about 4 minutes, until softened. Stir in the mustard seeds, cumin seeds, turmeric, fenugreek, curry leaves, garlic and chile; cook for about 1 minute, until the mustard seeds begin to pop.

2 Stir in the salt, pepper, carrots, lentils, spinach and broth. Secure the lid and cook on high pressure for 12 minutes.

3 Once the cooking is complete, let the pressure release naturally for 10 minutes, then quick-release the remaining pressure.

4 Remove the lid and stir in the cilantro. Taste and add more salt, if needed; serve.

NOTE *If you don't have spinach, you can use any fresh greens you have on hand, such as Swiss chard, kale, mustard greens, carrot or radish tops or beet greens.*

Turmeric Ginger GF
CHICKEN BROTH

Bone broth is everywhere these days, but it's been in India forever (like yoga, turmeric and call centers—am I the only one who thinks India is pulling the world's strings?). This is a really easy recipe to prep. You can buy bones from your butcher or simply freeze raw or roasted chicken bones, then pull them out when you want a to make a batch of bone broth in two hours rather than two days. Make sure you don't skip the lemon juice—the acid is what pulls the minerals out of the bones and makes this a healthy drink, snack or soup base. I like to add a few extra slices of ginger and makrut lime leaves to the broth when I drink it, especially if I am feeling run-down.

2   tablespoons (30 mL) **black peppercorns**, crushed

2   tablespoons (30 mL) **coriander seeds**

1   tablespoon (15 mL) **cumin seeds**

1   tablespoon (15 mL) ground **turmeric**

15 fresh **curry leaves**, torn into pieces

2   **serrano chiles**, chopped

2   **onions**, chopped

1   4-inch (10 cm) piece **ginger**, sliced

6   **garlic cloves**, peeled and smashed

3   pounds (1.5 kg) **chicken bones** (see Note)

2   **chicken feet** (optional)

¼   cup (60 mL) freshly squeezed **lemon juice**

    Water

    Kosher salt (optional)

1   Using the Sauté function on High, toast the peppercorns, coriander seeds, cumin seeds, turmeric and curry leaves in the inner pot, stirring, for 1 to 2 minutes, until fragrant. Add the chiles, onions, ginger, garlic, chicken bones, chicken feet (if using) and lemon juice. Pour enough water over the bones to cover them by 1 inch (2.5 cm); secure the lid.

2   Using the Soup function on Normal, cook the broth for 2 hours.

3   Once the cooking is complete, let the pressure release naturally.

4   Pour the broth through a fine-mesh sieve (or a colander lined with cheesecloth). Taste and add salt, if needed. Serve immediately or let cool and store in an airtight container in the refrigerator for up to 5 days.

NOTE *If you want to roast your chicken bones for a richer-flavored broth, place them on a rimmed baking sheet or roasting pan in an even layer. Roast at 375°F (190°C) for 15 minutes, until lightly browned.*

TOMATO *Saar*

VEG **GF** **V** (TANGY TOMATO SOUP)

This is a Mangalorean version of rasam, a soup from southern India that is thin but full of tangy and spicy flavors. The light tomato broth is perfect to sip on a hot day when you want something refreshing. Add a little cooked rice if you want to make it a more substantial dish.

Blender

2	tablespoons (30 mL) **vegetable oil**
10	fresh **curry leaves**, torn into pieces
2	teaspoons (10 mL) **cumin seeds**
2	teaspoons (10 mL) **coriander seeds**
¼	teaspoon (1 mL) **Kashmiri chili powder**
1	can (28 oz/796 mL) whole **tomatoes**, roughly chopped (see Note)
1	tablespoon (15 mL) freshly ground **black pepper**
1	teaspoon (5 mL) **kosher salt** (approx.)
3	cups (750 mL) **water**
2	tablespoons (30 mL) **tamarind concentrate** (see page 33) or freshly squeezed **lemon juice** (approx.)
1	tablespoon (15 mL) **jaggery** or **brown sugar** (approx.)

1 Using the Sauté function on High, heat the oil in the inner pot for about 1 minute, until shimmering. Add the curry leaves, cumin seeds, coriander seeds and chili powder; cook, stirring, for about 1 minute, until fragrant and the seeds begin to pop.

2 Add the tomatoes (with juice), pepper and salt.

3 Add the water, tamarind concentrate and jaggery; stir to combine. Secure the lid and cook, using the Soup function on Normal, for 5 minutes.

4 Once the cooking is complete, let the pressure release naturally for 10 minutes, then quick-release the remaining pressure.

5 Remove the lid and let cool slightly. Working in batches, transfer the soup to a blender. Blend on high speed until smooth. Season to taste with additional salt, tamarind juice or jaggery, if needed. I like to sip this soup from a mug.

NOTE *If tomatoes are in season, use 2 pounds (1 kg) whole tomatoes (the juicier the better) that have been roughly chopped, instead of the canned.*

LEMON
Rasam

 VEG GF V **(TART, PEPPERY BROTH)**

Rasam is very important to South Indians. A spicy broth, it's used as the base for a light meal with rice, and it also happens to be a surefire treatment for a cold or sore throat (never argue with aunties who say so). There are hundreds of different versions of this soup, which can be made using everything from pineapple to tomatoes to tamarind. Mine includes everything I love about rasam—it's peppery and tangy, light but satisfying.

Blender or mini food processor

½ cup (125 mL) dried **pigeon peas** (toor dal) or any **lentils**, rinsed

1 teaspoon (5 mL) ground **turmeric**, divided

Water

2 teaspoons (10 mL) **cumin seeds**

2 teaspoons (10 mL) **coriander seeds**

1 tablespoon (15 mL) freshly ground **black pepper**

1 2-inch (5 cm) piece **ginger**, chopped

1 **green Thai chile**, minced

4 large **garlic cloves**, chopped

1 teaspoon (5 mL) **vegetable oil**

1 teaspoon (5 mL) **yellow mustard seeds**

15 fresh **curry leaves**, torn into pieces

1 **dried red chile**, torn into pieces

¼ teaspoon (1 mL) **asafoetida** (optional)

½ teaspoon (2 mL) **kosher salt** (approx.)

¼ cup (60 mL) freshly squeezed **lemon juice** (approx.)

½ cup (125 mL) chopped fresh **cilantro**

1 Combine the pigeon peas, ½ teaspoon (2 mL) turmeric and 1 cup (250 mL) water in the inner pot. Secure the lid and cook on high pressure for 10 minutes.

2 Meanwhile, combine the cumin seeds, coriander seeds, pepper, ginger, green chile and garlic in a blender; blend on high speed into a thick paste.

3 Once the cooking is complete, let the pressure release naturally for 10 minutes, then quick-release the remaining pressure.

4 Using a wooden spoon or potato masher, mash the cooked peas; then transfer to a medium bowl. Clean the inner pot.

5 Using the Sauté function on High, heat the oil for about 1 minute, until shimmering. Add the mustard seeds, curry leaves, dried chile and remaining ½ teaspoon (2 mL) turmeric; cook for about 90 seconds, until the curry leaves are sizzling.

6 Add the ginger-garlic paste and asafoetida (if using); stir to combine. Add the cooked peas, 3 cups (750 mL) water and the salt; stir to combine. Cook for 10 minutes, until the flavors have melded. Stir in the lemon juice. Taste and add more salt and lemon juice, if needed. Garnish with cilantro; serve.

CHAPTER FIVE

VEGETABLES

Matar WITH FETA

  (STEWED PEAS AND CHEESE)

Traditional matar paneer—or peas and cheese, as we called it growing up—has a dark, rich tomato gravy and cubes of paneer amid a bowl of stewed peas. Think of this dish as traditional matar paneer's cousin who spent a summer backpacking through Greece. This version is light on the gravy so you taste more of the clean, sweet flavors of the peas, accentuated by the light, floral flavor of coriander. Cubed feta adds a little tanginess and the lemon and mint give it a green brightness, making this a colorful spring-y side dish for any meal.

2   tablespoons (30 mL) **ghee** or **coconut oil**

1   **onion**, minced

1   tablespoon (15 mL) ground **coriander**

1   tablespoon (15 mL) ground **cumin**

1   **serrano chile**, finely chopped

1   tablespoon (15 mL) grated **lemon zest** or minced **Saffron-Preserved Meyer Lemon** (page 76)

½   cup (125 mL) **water**

1   pound (500 g) frozen **peas**

7   ounces (210 g) **feta cheese**, cubed

¼   cup (60 mL) finely chopped **mint** leaves

1   Using the Sauté function on High, heat the ghee in the inner pot for about 1 minute, until shimmering. Add the onion and stir to combine. Add the coriander and cumin and cook, stirring occasionally, for about 3 minutes, until the onion has softened. Add the chile and cook, stirring occasionally, for 1 minute, until fragrant.

2   Stir in the lemon zest, water and peas. Secure the lid and cook on low pressure for 0 minutes. (Yes, really! This is a nice trick for cooking vegetables—the peas cook in the time it takes for the pressure to build. You can cook them on high pressure for the same amount of time, but you may risk overcooking the peas.)

3   Once the cooking is complete, quick-release the pressure.

4   Remove the lid and stir in the feta and chopped mint; serve.

SAAG PANEER

VEG · GF

(STEWED SPICED GREENS AND CHEESE)

The terms *saag paneer* and *palak paneer* are used almost interchangeably in a lot of Indian restaurants, but the two dishes actually use different types of greens. *Palak* features spinach and *saag* uses a mixture of greens. I like to blend mustard greens with spinach; they add a nice peppery note that punches everything up and keeps the flavors bright.

2 teaspoons (10 mL) ground **turmeric**

½ teaspoon (2 mL) **Kashmiri chili powder**

1½ teaspoons (7 mL) **kosher salt**, divided (approx.)

8 ounces (250 g) **Firm Paneer** (page 68) or store-bought, cubed

¼ cup (60 mL) **ghee** or **vegetable oil**, divided

1 **onion**, chopped

2 teaspoons (10 mL) **Garam Masala** (page 24) or store-bought

1 teaspoon (5 mL) ground **cumin**

½ teaspoon (2 mL) ground **nutmeg**

3 tablespoons (45 mL) minced **garlic**

2 tablespoons (30 mL) minced **ginger**

2 **serrano chiles**, minced

½ cup (125 mL) **water**

2 cups (500 mL) chopped **mustard greens** or **kale**

1 package (10 oz/300 g) frozen chopped **spinach** (see Note)

2 tablespoons (30 mL) **butter**

½ cup (125 mL) **heavy** or **whipping** (35%) **cream** (optional)

1 tablespoon (15 mL) **red pepper flakes**

NOTE *If you would rather use fresh spinach, substitute 1 pound (500 g) fresh spinach for the frozen.*

1   Combine the turmeric, chili powder and ½ teaspoon (2 mL) salt in a medium bowl. Add the paneer and toss to coat.

2   Using the Sauté function on High, heat 2 tablespoons (30 mL) ghee in the inner pot for about 1 minute, until shimmering. Add the paneer; cook for about 5 minutes, turning occasionally, until browned on each side. Return the paneer to the bowl; keep the Sauté function turned on.

3   Heat the remaining 2 tablespoons (30 mL) ghee in the inner pot. Add the onion; cook, stirring occasionally, for about 4 minutes, until softened. Stir in the garam masala, cumin, nutmeg, remaining 1 teaspoon (5 mL) salt, garlic, ginger and chiles; cook for about 1 minute, until fragrant.

4   Add the water and stir with a wooden spoon, scraping up any browned bits on the bottom of the pot. Add the mustard greens and cook for about 1 minute, until somewhat wilted. Add the frozen spinach. Secure the lid and cook on high pressure for 8 minutes.

5   Once the cooking is complete, quick-release the pressure.

6   Remove the lid and stir (the spinach will have retained its block shape but will fall apart immediately). If you prefer a smooth texture, purée the greens with an immersion blender. Stir in the butter, cream (if using) and red pepper flakes; taste and add more salt, if needed. Stir in the paneer, transfer to a platter and serve.

CORN KI SUBZI

  (SWEET CURRIED CREAMED CORN)

Think of this dish as an Indian-style creamed corn, inspired by the corn dishes from Gujarat, in the western part of India. It's a terrific side dish for an Indian-American barbecue; I like to serve it with Bafat Pork Ribs (page 221) and Sweet Potato Pav Bhaji (page 118). I've also been known to eat it straight from the bowl with tortilla chips—it's a great dip as well as a side dish.

- 2 teaspoons (10 mL) **vegetable oil**
- 1 **onion**, chopped
- 2 teaspoons (10 mL) minced **ginger**
- 1 teaspoon (5 mL) ground **cumin**
- 2 teaspoons (10 mL) ground **turmeric**
- 6 fresh **curry leaves**, torn into pieces
- 2 teaspoons (10 mL) **kosher salt** (approx.)
- 2 teaspoons (10 mL) minced **garlic**
- 2 teaspoons (10 mL) minced **green Thai chiles**
- 3 cups (750 mL) fresh or frozen **corn**
- 1 cup (250 mL) **heavy** or **whipping** (35%) **cream**
- ¼ cup (60 mL) chopped **cilantro**

1 Using the Sauté function on High, heat the oil in the inner pot for about 1 minute, until shimmering. Add the onion and cook, stirring occasionally, for about 4 minutes, until the onion has softened.

2 Stir in the ginger, cumin, turmeric, curry leaves, salt, garlic and chiles; cook for about 1 minute, until fragrant. Stir in the corn and cream. Secure the lid and cook on low pressure for 10 minutes (you can also cook on high pressure for 5 minutes).

3 Once the cooking is complete, quick-release the pressure.

4 Remove the lid, taste and add more salt, if needed. Stir in the cilantro; serve.

GUNPOWDER
POTATOES

VEG **GF** (SMASHED POTATOES)

Easily about half the time I tell people I am writing an Indian cookbook, they tell me how much they love the potatoes from the restaurant Dishoom in London. I don't know when my friends became so cosmopolitan, but as soon as I tried the recipe created by Dishoom chef Navid Nasir, I understood the chatter and quickly adapted the dish for the Instant Pot. With their crispy outside and soft center, these potatoes are like a hybrid of roast potatoes and French fries—is there anything better?

1 pound (500 g) **yellow-fleshed potatoes**, quartered

1 cup (250 mL) **water**

5 tablespoons (75 mL) **ghee** or **vegetable oil**, divided

1 teaspoon (5 mL) ground **cumin**

1 teaspoon (5 mL) **fennel seeds**

1 teaspoon (5 mL) ground **coriander**

1 teaspoon (5 mL) **Kashmiri chili powder**

1 teaspoon (5 mL) **Chaat Masala** (page 25) or store-bought

1 teaspoon (5 mL) ground **fenugreek**

1 teaspoon (5 mL) ground **turmeric**

1 teaspoon (5 mL) **kosher salt**

1 **green Thai chile**, minced

4 **garlic cloves**, minced

2 tablespoons (30 mL) freshly squeezed **lime juice**

¼ cup (60 mL) minced **cilantro**

1 Preheat the oven to 375°F (190°C).

2 Place the potatoes and water in the inner pot. Secure the lid and cook on low pressure for 12 minutes (you can also cook on high pressure for 8 minutes).

3 Once the cooking is complete, quick-release the pressure.

4 Discard water and transfer the potatoes to a baking sheet. Let the potatoes cool for about 5 minutes. Using a fork or a potato masher, gently smash into flattened disks.

5 Using the Sauté function on High, heat ¼ cup (60 mL) ghee in the inner pot for about 1 minute, until shimmering. Stir in the cumin, fennel seeds, coriander, chili powder, chaat masala, fenugreek, turmeric, salt, chile and garlic; cook for about 1 minute, until the spices are fragrant. Pour the spiced ghee mixture over the potatoes.

6 Roast the potatoes in the preheated oven for 15 minutes, until crispy. Transfer to a platter and drizzle the lime juice and remaining 1 tablespoon (15 mL) ghee overtop. Sprinkle with cilantro and serve.

Punjabi-Style PUMPKIN CURRY

VEG · GF · V

This cooked pumpkin with warm, wintery spices comes from the Punjab region of India, in the north; it is similar to the spiced pumpkin or winter squash often served with Rogan Ghosh (page 219) in New Delhi. Back home in America I like to eat this with a Sunday roast or, especially, as part of my Thanksgiving dinner. Give the candied yams with marshmallows the boot and try this with any big holiday meal.

- 1 tablespoon (15 mL) **vegetable oil**
- 1 teaspoon (5 mL) **yellow mustard seeds**
- 1 teaspoon (5 mL) **cumin seeds**
- ½ teaspoon (2 mL) **fenugreek seeds**
- 1 pound (500 g) **sweet pumpkin**, peeled, seeded and cubed
- 1 teaspoon (5 mL) **Kashmiri chili powder**
- 2 teaspoons (10 mL) **kosher salt**
- 1 teaspoon (5 mL) **amchur powder** or **ground sumac**
- 1 teaspoon (5 mL) ground **turmeric**
- 1 teaspoon (5 mL) **Garam Masala** (page 24) or store-bought
- 1 tablespoon (15 mL) **jaggery** or **brown sugar**
- 1 tablespoon (15 mL) minced **ginger**
- 1 cup (250 mL) **water**

1 Using the Sauté function on High, heat the oil in the inner pot for about 1 minute, until shimmering. Add the mustard seeds, cumin seeds and fenugreek seeds; cook for about 1 minute, until the mustard seeds begin to pop.

2 Add the pumpkin and stir to combine. Stir in the chili powder, salt, amchur, turmeric, garam masala, jaggery and ginger; cook for about 1 minute, until fragrant. Stir in the water, using a wooden spoon to scrape up any browned bits from the bottom of the pot. Secure the lid and cook on high pressure for 4 minutes.

3 Once the cooking is complete, quick-release the pressure.

4 Remove the lid and stir the pumpkin and spices; serve.

BOMBAY-STYLE Shakshuka

  VEG **GF** (EGGS POACHED IN SPICED TOMATO AND PEPPERS)

No, shakshuka is not Indian, but stay with me here. The Persian community in Bombay popularized this dish of eggs cooked in tomatoes, and it's still available in cafés all over the city. This version is warm with garam masala, Kashmiri chili powder and other Indian spices, making it ideal for any breakfast-for-dinner situation.

2 tablespoons (30 mL) **ghee** or **vegetable oil**

2 **onions**, sliced

2 teaspoons (10 mL) ground **coriander**

1 teaspoon (5 mL) ground **cumin**

1 teaspoon (5 mL) **Garam Masala** (page 24) or store-bought

1 teaspoon (5 mL) **Kashmiri chili powder**

1 teaspoon (5 mL) ground **turmeric**

2 teaspoons (10 mL) minced **ginger**

4 **garlic cloves**, minced

1 can (28 oz/796 mL) whole **tomatoes** (with juice), roughly chopped

Kosher salt

1 teaspoon (5 mL) freshly ground **black pepper**

1 teaspoon (5 mL) granulated **sugar** (optional)

3 cups (750 mL) chopped **spinach** leaves

½ cup (125 mL) chopped **cilantro**, divided

6 large **eggs**

1 cup (250 mL) **Plain Yogurt** (page 40) or store-bought

Naan (optional)

Cooked **lentils** (optional)

1 Using the Sauté function on High, heat the ghee in the inner pot until shimmering, about 1 minute. Add the onions and cook, stirring, for about 4 minutes, until softened. Stir in the coriander, cumin, garam masala, chili powder and turmeric; cook for about 1 minute, until fragrant. Stir in the ginger and garlic; cook for about 1 minute, until fragrant.

2 Add the tomatoes (with juice); using a wooden spoon, stir, scraping up any browned bits on the bottom of the pot. Stir in 1 teaspoon (5 mL) salt and the pepper. Secure the lid and cook on high pressure for 10 minutes.

3 Once the cooking is complete, let the pressure release naturally for 5 minutes, then quick-release the remaining pressure.

4 Remove the lid and taste the sauce; add the sugar (if using). Stir in the spinach and cilantro, then make 6 indentions in the sauce with the back of a ladle. Crack one egg into a small bowl, then tip it into a divot and sprinkle with additional salt. Repeat with remaining eggs.

5 Secure the lid and cook on low pressure for 1 minute (see Note). Once the cooking is complete, quick-release the pressure. If you want the eggs to be a little more cooked, place the lid on top of the pot while it's still warm and let stand for 1 or 2 minutes.

6 Serve with yogurt and/or naan and cooked lentils (if using).

NOTE *If your machine does not have a low-pressure setting, set the pressure to High for 1 minute instead. Release the pressure after 5 minutes, even if the machine has not yet pressurized.*

NAVRATAN KORMA

VEG **GF** **V** (RICH, CREAMY VEGETABLE STEW)

This is a super-rich, stick-to-your-ribs vegetable dish, named for the nine "jewels" (actually courtiers) of Akbar, a Mughal emperor. Traditional navratan korma recipes call for either nine vegetables or nine garnishes, but that's a lot to prepare by anyone's standards (unless you are an emperor and have nine servants cooking your dinner, in which case, you do you). I use a total of nine vegetables and garnishes just to stay on the safe side, karma-wise.

High-powered blender or food processor

- 1 cup (250 mL) raw **cashews**
  Water
- ¼ cup (60 mL) sliced **ginger**
- 8 **garlic cloves**
- 1 large **onion**, roughly chopped
- 3 tablespoons (45 mL) **vegetable oil**

- 1 teaspoon (5 mL) ground **cardamom**
- 1 teaspoon (5 mL) ground **cloves**
- ½ teaspoon (2 mL) ground **cinnamon**
- 1 **serrano chile**, minced
- 1 teaspoon (5 mL) ground **turmeric**
- 1 teaspoon (5 mL) **Kashmiri chili powder**
- 1 tablespoon (15 mL) **kosher salt** (approx.)
- 1 cup (250 mL) **cauliflower florets** (1-inch/2.5 cm pieces)
- 2 **carrots**, cut into ½-inch (1 cm) slices
- 2 **yellow-fleshed potatoes**, cut into 1-inch (2.5 cm) pieces
- 1 **red bell pepper**, cut into 1-inch (2.5 cm) pieces
- 2 cups (500 mL) frozen **peas**, thawed
- 1 cup (250 mL) toasted raw **cashews** (see page 32)
- ¾ cup (175 mL) minced **cilantro**

1   Place the raw cashews in a medium bowl. Add 1½ cups (375 mL) water to cover; soak at room temperature for 2 hours. Drain and rinse.

2   Combine the drained cashews and 1 cup (250 mL) fresh water in a blender or food processor; blend on high speed into a smooth paste, adding more water as needed to achieve a paste consistency. Return the paste to the bowl.

3   Place the ginger, garlic and onion in the blender (you don't need to clean it out); blend on high speed until smooth and watery. Transfer the mixture to a small bowl.

4   Using the Sauté function on High, heat the oil in the inner pot for about 1 minute, until shimmering. Add the cardamom, cloves and cinnamon; cook for about 30 seconds, until fragrant. Add the ginger-garlic paste and the chile; cook, stirring constantly, for about 1 minute, until fragrant. Add the cashew paste; cook, stirring constantly, for about 2 minutes, until well combined with the other ingredients. Stir in the turmeric, chili powder and salt.

5   Add the cauliflower, carrots, potatoes and bell pepper. Secure the lid and cook on low pressure for 10 minutes (you can also cook on high pressure for 6 minutes).

6   Once the cooking is complete, quick-release the pressure.

7   Remove the lid and stir in the peas. Using the Sauté function on Normal, cook, stirring occasionally, for 2 to 3 minutes, until creamy and thick. Taste and add more salt, if needed. Transfer to a serving dish and top with the toasted cashews and cilantro; serve.

Bengali VEG GF CARROTS

I wasn't familiar with the spice blend panch phoron until my cousin Neeru pointed it out while we were in an Indian grocery store together. It's since become one of the most popular players in my spice drawer. Panch phoron is known as Bengali five-spice and is a combination of some of my favorite spice seeds: cumin, brown or yellow mustard, fenugreek, nigella and fennel. Neeru's mother uses it on carrots, so I copied that idea to come up with this dish.

1 cup (250 mL) cooked **chickpeas**

3 tablespoons (45 mL) **ghee** or **butter**, divided

1 teaspoon (5 mL) ground **cumin**

1 pound (500 g) **carrots**, cut into 3-inch (7.5 cm) pieces

2 teaspoons (10 mL) **kosher salt**, divided

2 teaspoons (10 mL) **Panch Phoron** (page 26) or store-bought

½ cup (125 mL) **Plain Yogurt** (page 40) or store-bought

2 tablespoons (30 mL) minced **cilantro**

1 Preheat the oven to 375°F (190°C).

2 Combine the chickpeas, 1 tablespoon (15 mL) ghee and cumin in a large bowl; toss to coat.

3 Spread out the chickpeas on a baking sheet; bake in the preheated oven for about 15 minutes, until crispy.

4 Using the Sauté function on High, heat the remaining 2 tablespoons (30 mL) ghee for about 1 minute, until shimmering. Add the carrots and 1 teaspoon (5 mL) salt; cook, stirring occasionally, for about 7 minutes, until lightly browned.

5 Secure the lid and cook on high pressure for 1 minute.

6 Once the cooking is complete, quick-release the pressure.

7 Remove the lid and add the panch phoron. Using the Sauté function on High, cook for 1 minute, until the spices are toasted.

8 Transfer the carrots to a platter (make sure you scoop out all the seeds too) and garnish with yogurt, crispy chickpeas and cilantro; serve.

NOTE *If you have any raita sitting around, go ahead and use it on the carrots instead of the plain yogurt.*

COCONUT
GREEN
BEANS

VEG · GF · V

You probably don't expect crisp, bright green beans from an Instant Pot, but not everything cooked in this machine needs to be braised into submission. Case in point: these lemony green beans doused in ginger and coconut and ready in no time. I like how this dish adds a nice contrast to all the stewed meats and vegetables in this book, especially Bafat Pork Ribs (page 221).

3 tablespoons (45 mL) **vegetable oil** or **coconut oil**

2 teaspoons (10 mL) **cumin seeds**

1 **dried red chile**, crushed

1 teaspoon (5 mL) **yellow mustard seeds**

2 tablespoons (30 mL) minced **ginger**

4 **garlic cloves**, minced

1 cup (250 mL) unsweetened **coconut flakes**

1½ teaspoons (7 mL) **kosher salt** (approx.)

½ cup (125 mL) **water**

1½ pounds (750 g) **green beans**, trimmed

½ **lemon**

1 Using the Sauté function on High, heat the oil in the inner pot for about 1 minute, until shimmering. Add the cumin seeds, chile and mustard seeds; cook for about 1 minute, until the seeds begin to pop. Stir in the ginger, garlic and coconut; cook for about 1 minute, until fragrant.

2 Stir in the salt, water and beans. Secure the lid and cook on low pressure for 1 minute. (You can also cook on high pressure for 0 minutes—the beans will cook in the time it takes for the pressure to build.)

3 Once the cooking is complete, quick-release the pressure.

4 Remove the lid and stir to combine. Squeeze the lemon over the beans. Taste and add more salt, if needed. Serve.

PORRIDGE

and

RICE

COCONUT Upma

VEG V (SEMOLINA PORRIDGE)

Upma is a traditional South Indian breakfast porridge made with roasted semolina. It's like a savory Cream of Wheat, but it's easy to adapt to whatever mood you are in, whether sweet or savory. This version has a little spice, but sometimes I switch it up and stir in some brown sugar and dried cherries or raisins instead, to make a sweet upma. You can add whatever you like to create your own ideal breakfast bowl.

4 tablespoons (60 mL) **coconut oil** or **vegetable oil**, divided

1 **onion**, chopped

1 **serrano chile**, minced

1 tablespoon (15 mL) minced **ginger**

3 cups (750 mL) **water**

¼ cup (60 mL) unsweetened **coconut flakes**

1 cup (250 mL) grated **carrots**

2 teaspoons (10 mL) **kosher salt**

2 cups (500 mL) toasted **rava** or **semolina** (see Note)

2 teaspoons (10 mL) **lime juice**

½ cup (125 mL) **cashew pieces**

6 fresh **curry leaves**, torn into pieces

1 teaspoon (5 mL) **brown mustard seeds**

1 Using the Sauté function on High, heat 2 tablespoons (30 mL) oil in the inner pot for about 1 minute, until shimmering. Add the onion, chile and ginger; cook, stirring occasionally, for about 4 minutes, until the onion has softened.

2 Stir in the water, coconut, carrots, salt and rava. Secure the lid and cook on high pressure for 1 minute.

3 Once the cooking is complete, quick-release the pressure.

4 Remove the lid and stir in the lime juice. Turn off the Instant Pot, secure the lid, and let it stand for 5 minutes as the upma steams a bit in the residual heat.

5 Meanwhile, heat the remaining 2 tablespoons (30 mL) oil in a medium skillet over medium heat. Add the cashews and cook, stirring constantly, for about 2 minutes, until lightly browned. Add the curry leaves and mustard seeds; cook for about 1 minute, until the leaves sizzle and the seeds pop. Stir in a pinch of salt and remove the pan from the heat.

6 Transfer the upma to bowls and garnish with the toasted cashew mixture; serve.

NOTE *It's easy to toast rava or semolina at home if you can't find pre-toasted. Just add the rava or semolina to a small, dry skillet over medium heat. Cook, stirring constantly, for about 3 to 4 minutes, until pale brown. Immediately transfer to a bowl and let cool before using.*

CARDAMOM
JAGGERY VEG V
OATMEAL

When I was a kid, my parents would ship a giant box of American food—think canned tuna, pancake mix, instant oatmeal—to my grandparents' house before each visit to India, so that my brothers and I would have some familiar food to eat (and to appease our bratty American palates). But the reality that we weren't in Kentucky anymore set in when our oatmeal was made with yak milk delivered in a plastic bag, still warm from the source (which was loitering nearby at the side of the road). On the positive side, it was topped with large grains of demerara sugar, which kind of made up for the yak milk. But my Irish mother would always shake her head at our thin, watery gruel; she knew that real oatmeal was richer, thicker stuff. This steel-cut oatmeal with a hint of cardamom is both of my cultures in one bowl.

1½ cups (375 mL) **steel-cut oats**

1 teaspoon (5 mL) ground **cardamom** (approx.)

1 cup (250 mL) full-fat **coconut milk** (approx.)

2 cups (500 mL) **water**

¼ cup (60 mL) **jaggery** or **brown sugar**

½ teaspoon (2 mL) **kosher salt**

1 teaspoon (5 mL) minced **ginger**

½ teaspoon (2 mL) ground **cinnamon**

1   Using the Sauté function on Normal, toast the oats and cardamom in the inner pot, stirring frequently, for about 2 minutes, until fragrant.

2   Stir in the coconut milk, water, jaggery, salt and ginger. Secure the lid and cook on high pressure for 3 minutes.

3   Once the cooking is complete, let the pressure release naturally.

4   Remove the lid and stir. If you want the oats to be softer, use the Sauté function to simmer the oatmeal with additional coconut milk or water, until you reach your preferred consistency. Sprinkle with cinnamon; serve.

NOTE   *You can customize this recipe in a number of ways. I sometimes add dried fruit or chopped bananas to the oatmeal before or after cooking, or stir in some nuts or almond butter after it's cooked.*

COCONUT CILANTRO
RICE PILAF

This super-simple basic pilaf is a step above plain rice. The coconut and ginger add bright flavors and pair especially well with South Indian recipes that also use coconut, like Goan Shrimp Curry (page 230).

1   cup (250 mL) **white basmati rice**

1¾ cups (425 mL) **water**, divided

¾   cup (175 mL) full-fat **coconut milk**

1   tablespoon (15 mL) minced **ginger**

1   teaspoon (5 mL) **kosher salt**

¼   cup (60 mL) minced fresh **cilantro**

1   Place the rice in a medium bowl and cover with 1 cup (250 mL) water. Let stand for 20 minutes, then drain and rinse.

2   Place the rice, remaining ¾ cup (175 mL) water, coconut milk, ginger and salt in the inner pot. Secure the lid and cook on high pressure for 3 minutes.

3   Once the cooking is complete, let the pressure release naturally for 10 minutes, then quick-release the remaining pressure.

4   Remove the lid and add the cilantro. Fluff the rice with a fork, distributing the cilantro evenly; serve.

SAUTÉ	MANUAL	RELEASE	TOTAL	SERVES
3 MIN	**3 MIN**	**NATURAL/ QUICK**	**25 MIN** (PLUS 20 MIN TO SOAK)	**6 TO 8**

PRESERVED LEMON
JEERA
RICE

VEG · GF · V

(BASMATI RICE WITH CUMIN)

This rice combines two of my favorite ingredients, lemon and cumin. It's a nice, slightly upgraded everyday rice that goes with just about everything, from Saag Paneer (page 142) to Chana Masala (page 198).

2 cups (500 mL) white **basmati rice**

4 cups (1 L) **water**, divided

2 tablespoons (30 mL) **vegetable oil**

2 tablespoons (30 mL) **cumin seeds**

½ **Saffron-Preserved Meyer Lemon** (page 76) or store-bought **preserved lemon**, rinsed and finely chopped (see Note)

1 teaspoon (5 mL) **kosher salt**

1 Place the rice in a medium bowl and cover with 2 cups (500 mL) water. Let stand for 20 minutes, then drain and rinse.

2 Using the Sauté function on High, heat the oil in the inner pot for about 1 minute, until shimmering. Add the cumin seeds and cook for about 1 minute, until sizzling. Add the rice; cook, stirring constantly, for 1 minute. Stir in the remaining 2 cups (500 mL) water, preserved lemon and salt. Secure the lid and cook on high pressure for 3 minutes.

3 Once the cooking is complete, let the pressure release naturally for 10 minutes, then quick-release the remaining pressure.

4 Remove the lid, fluff the rice and serve.

NOTE *If you don't have any preserved lemons, mince half a seeded lemon, place in a food processor with 1 teaspoon (5 mL) apple cider vinegar, and process until smooth. It's an easy substitute when you're preserved lemon–deprived.*

SAUTÉ	MANUAL	RELEASE	TOTAL	SERVES
8 MIN	**3 MIN**	**NATURAL/ QUICK**	**30 MIN** (PLUS 20 MIN TO SOAK)	**6 TO 8**

VEG GF V SAFFRON
PULAO

(SPICED RICE WITH DRIED APRICOTS AND NUTS)

Pulao is a rice dish that is somewhere between a pilaf and a biryani. For this version, I mix in spices, nuts and dried fruit, giving it a hint of sweetness that sets it apart from a lot of the rice dishes you usually find in India. It's a simple preparation that can also stand on its own as an easy light meal.

2 cups (500 mL) **white basmati rice**

4 cups (1 L) **water**, divided

2 tablespoons (30 mL) **coconut oil** or **vegetable oil**

¼ cup (60 mL) chopped raw **hazelnuts**, **pecans** or **cashews**

¼ cup (60 mL) chopped **dried apricots**

Pinch ground **cinnamon**

1 **onion**, thinly sliced

2 teaspoons (10 mL) **Garam Masala** (page 24) or store-bought

1 teaspoon (5 mL) ground **cumin**

1 teaspoon (5 mL) **kosher salt**

1 **carrot**, chopped

Large pinch **saffron**

1 2-inch (5 cm) **cinnamon stick**

¼ cup (60 mL) minced fresh **cilantro**

¼ cup (60 mL) minced fresh **mint** leaves

1 Place the rice in a medium bowl and cover with 2 cups (500 mL) water. Let stand for 20 minutes, then drain and rinse.

2 Using the Sauté function on High, heat the oil in the inner pot for about 1 minute, until shimmering. Add the nuts, apricots and ground cinnamon; cook, stirring, for 2 minutes, until toasted and fragrant. Transfer the nuts to a bowl.

3 Add the onion to the inner pot; cook, stirring occasionally, for about 4 minutes, until softened. Stir in the garam masala, cumin and salt; cook for about 1 minute, until fragrant. Add the carrot, saffron, cinnamon stick, rice and remaining 2 cups (500 mL) water. Secure the lid and cook on high pressure for 3 minutes.

4 Once the cooking is complete, let the pressure release naturally for 10 minutes, then quick-release the remaining pressure.

5 Remove the lid, fluff the rice and stir in the reserved nuts and apricots, cilantro and mint; serve.

NOTE *You can play around with this dish by adding root vegetables (celery root is especially nice here) or other nuts or dried fruit that you have on hand.*

YOGURT RICE

VEG **GF**

Don't let the title of the recipe fool you—this dish is so much more than the sum of its parts. Here rice is mixed with yogurt and then doused with a tempering of nuts, dal, curry leaves, chiles and spices cooked in oil. It's a classic South Indian lunch dish for a hot day, and one of my favorite ways to use leftover rice (see Note). Cook the rice until it is a bit mushy and somewhat overcooked; that's the texture you want for this dish (don't ask why— it's a South Indian thing).

1½ cups (375 mL) **white basmati rice**, rinsed

2 cups (500 mL) **water**

2 teaspoons (10 mL) **kosher salt**

½ cup (125 mL) **milk**, warmed

2 cups (500 mL) **Plain Yogurt** (page 40) or store-bought

1 tablespoon (15 mL) **vegetable oil**

1 tablespoon (15 mL) dried **lentils**, rinsed

3 tablespoons (45 mL) crushed raw **cashews** or **peanuts**

2 **green Thai chiles**, minced

1 tablespoon (15 mL) unsweetened **coconut flakes**

1 tablespoon (15 mL) minced **ginger**

1 dried **red chile**, torn into pieces

1 teaspoon (5 mL) **yellow mustard seeds**

8 fresh **curry leaves**, torn into pieces

Pinch **asafoetida** (optional)

1 Combine the rice, water and salt in the inner pot. Secure the lid and cook using the Rice function (the machine will automatically set the cooking time to 12 minutes).

2 Once the cooking is complete, let the pressure release naturally for 10 minutes, then quick-release the remaining pressure.

3 Remove the lid and stir in the milk. Using a wooden spoon, gently mash the rice until the texture resembles rice pudding. Let it cool completely, then stir in the yogurt. Transfer to a large bowl.

4 Meanwhile, heat the oil in a medium skillet over medium heat. Add the lentils and nuts; cook for about 2 minutes, until just beginning to brown. Add the green chiles, coconut, ginger, dried chile, mustard seeds and curry leaves; cook for about 1 minute, until the mustard seeds begin to pop and the curry leaves sizzle. Add the asafoetida (if using), stir and remove from the heat. Pour the spice mixture over the yogurt rice and serve on a hot day.

NOTE *If you are using leftover cooked rice, start with Step 3.*

VEG GF V Spiced CONGEE

Many people think that congee, a rice porridge, is found only in China, where ingredients such as onions, tofu, dried fish and soy sauce will appear in the dish. It's eaten in India as well, and like its Chinese counterpart, depends on boldly flavored ingredients to take it from utterly plain to exciting. I think of congee as a somewhat neutral base, like polenta. Here it gets a simple spice-and-nut tempering inspired by Chinese Spicy Chili Crisp sauce, but you can use it as a base for any rich, saucy braised meats or vegetables.

1	cup (250 mL) **white basmati rice**, rinsed
1	tablespoon (15 mL) **kosher salt**
2	teaspoons (10 mL) minced **garlic**
2	teaspoons (10 mL) minced **ginger**
7	cups (1.75 L) **water**
¼	cup (60 mL) **ghee**
½	cup (125 mL) raw **cashew pieces**
6	fresh **curry leaves**, torn into pieces
10	**dried red chiles**, crushed
1	teaspoon (5 mL) **cumin seeds**
2	teaspoons (10 mL) **yellow mustard seeds**
¼	cup (60 mL) minced fresh **cilantro**

1 Place the rice, salt, garlic and ginger in the inner pot, then add the water. Secure the lid and cook using the Porridge function (the machine will automatically set the cooking time for 20 minutes).

2 Once the cooking is complete, let the pressure release naturally.

3 Meanwhile, heat the ghee in a medium skillet over medium heat. Add the cashews and toss to coat. Cook, shaking the pan, until the nuts are lightly toasted. Add the curry leaves, chiles, cumin seeds and mustard seeds; cook for about 1 minute, until the mustard seeds begin to pop and the curry leaves sizzle. Remove from the heat.

4 Transfer the congee to a serving bowl. Garnish with the cashew-spice mixture and cilantro; serve.

NOTE *Sometimes I double the quantities for the cashew-spice mixture in Step 3 and keep half in the fridge for spicing-things-up emergencies. It keeps for up to 1 month.*

CAULIFLOWER KALE
KITCHEREE

   (VEGETABLE, RICE AND LENTIL STEW)

Gently spiced, this wintery kitcheree is pure comfort food on a cold night. Adding cauliflower and kale makes this dish a really satisfying vegetarian meal. Feel free to add chopped root vegetables, Brussels sprouts or even beets.

1 cup (250 mL) **white basmati rice**

1 cup (250 mL) mixed dried **lentils** (moong, masoor or toor dal)

5 cups (1.25 mL) **water**, divided

2 tablespoons (30 mL) **vegetable oil** or coconut oil

2 tablespoons (30 mL) minced **ginger**

2 tablespoons (30 mL) minced **garlic**

1 teaspoon (5 mL) **cumin seeds**

1 teaspoon (5 mL) ground **turmeric**

1 small head **cauliflower**, chopped into 1-inch (2.5 cm) pieces

3 cups (750 mL) chopped trimmed **kale**

1 tablespoon (15 mL) **kosher salt**

½ cup (125 mL) chopped fresh **cilantro**

1 Place the rice and lentils in a medium bowl and cover with 2 cups (500 mL) water. Let stand for 20 minutes, then drain and rinse.

2 Using the Sauté function on High, heat the oil in the inner pot for about 1 minute, until shimmering. Stir in the ginger, garlic, cumin seeds and turmeric; cook for about 1 minute, until fragrant. Add the cauliflower, kale, rice, lentils and salt. Stir in the 3 cups (750 mL) water. Secure the lid and cook on high pressure for 5 minutes.

3 Once the cooking is complete, let the pressure release naturally for 5 minutes, then quick-release the remaining pressure.

4 Remove the lid. Transfer the kitcheree to a bowl and garnish with the cilantro; serve.

SPRING VEGETABLE
KITCHEREE

 **VEG** **GF** **V** (ASPARAGUS, RICE AND LENTIL STEW)

Kitcheree is classic Indian comfort-food dish of rice and moong dal, often served to help settle the stomach. This is a very light version, reminiscent of a spring risotto but with enough spices to remind you that its heart is still in India. Use the thinnest asparagus you can find for this dish, which I like to pair with a floral white wine for dinner in the first hopeful days of spring.

1	cup (250 mL) **white basmati rice**
1	cup (250 mL) mixed dried **lentils** (masoor or toor dal)
3	cups (750 mL) **water**, divided
2	tablespoons (30 mL) **coconut oil** or **vegetable oil**
2	tablespoons (30 mL) minced **ginger**
2	tablespoons (30 mL) minced **garlic**
1	teaspoon (5 mL) **cumin seeds**
1	teaspoon (5 mL) ground **coriander**
2	teaspoons (10 mL) **kosher salt**
2	cups (500 mL) green **peas**, thawed if frozen
4	cups (1 L) chopped **spinach**
1	pound (500 g) **asparagus**, trimmed and thinly sliced
2	tablespoons (30 mL) grated **lemon zest**
¼	cup (60 mL) minced fresh **herbs** (mint, dill, basil, or parsley)

1 Place the rice and lentils in a medium bowl and cover with 2 cups (500 mL) water. Let stand for 20 minutes, then drain and rinse.

2 Using the Sauté function on High, heat the oil in the inner pot for about 1 minute, until shimmering. Add the ginger, garlic, cumin seeds and coriander; cook, stirring, for about 1 minute, until fragrant. Add the rice, lentils and salt. Stir in the remaining 1 cup (250 mL) water and secure the lid. Cook on high pressure for 3 minutes.

3 Once the cooking is complete, let the pressure release naturally for 10 minutes, then quick-release the remaining pressure.

4 Remove the lid and stir in the peas, spinach, asparagus and lemon zest. Secure the lid again and let the vegetables steam in the residual heat for 3 minutes. Transfer the kitcheree to a serving bowl and garnish with the herbs; serve.

BISIBELABATH

   (SPICED RICE AND LENTILS)

Bisibelabath is kitcheree's spicier cousin. The name means "hot lentil rice," so consider yourself warned — this is a spicy dish of vegetables, rice and lentils, straight out of South India. I like to serve it with raita to cool things off.

Coffee/spice grinder

- 2 tablespoons (30 mL) **vegetable oil**, divided
- 2 tablespoons (30 mL) unsweetened **coconut flakes**
- 1½ tablespoons (22 mL) **coriander seeds**
- 1½ tablespoons (22 mL) dried **chana dal**
- 5 **black peppercorns**
  Pinch **fenugreek seeds**
- 1 2-inch (5 cm) **cinnamon stick**
- 3 whole **cloves**
  Pinch **asafoetida** (optional)
- 1 **dried red chile**, crushed
- 1 **onion**, chopped
- 1 tablespoon (15 mL) **kosher salt**
- 2 **green chiles**, minced
- 2 teaspoons (10 mL) ground **turmeric**
- 1 teaspoon (5 mL) **yellow mustard seeds**
- 1 cup (250 mL) **white basmati rice**, rinsed
- 1 cup (250 mL) dried **lentils** (toor or masoor dal)
- 2 cups (500 mL) chopped trimmed **acorn** or **butternut squash**
- 2 cups (500 mL) chopped **mustard greens** (see Note)
- 2 cups (500 mL) no-added-salt **vegetable broth** or **water**

1 Using the Sauté function on High, heat 1 teaspoon (5 mL) oil in the inner pot for 1 minute, until shimmering. Add the coconut, coriander seeds, chana dal, peppercorns, fenugreek seeds, cinnamon stick, cloves, asafoetida (if using) and dried chile; cook for about 2 minutes, until fragrant. Transfer the mixture to a clean coffee/spice grinder and grind to a powder.

2 Using the Sauté function on High, heat the remaining 5 teaspoons (25 mL) oil in the inner pot for 1 minute, until shimmering. Add the onion, salt, green chiles, turmeric and mustard seeds; cook for about 2 minutes, until the mustard seeds begin to pop. Add the rice, lentils, squash, and mustard greens; stir to combine. Stir in the broth. Secure the lid and cook on high pressure for 3 minutes.

3 Once the cooking is complete, let the pressure release naturally for 10 minutes, then quick-release the remaining pressure.

4 Remove the lid and stir. Transfer to a bowl; serve.

NOTE *If you can't find mustard greens, use turnip greens, kale or any other sturdy greens.*

CHAPTER SEVEN

BIRYANIS

VEGETABLE PANEER BIRYANI 176
(Rice with Vegetables and Cheese)

HYDERABADI BIRYANI 179
(Spicy Rice with Chicken)

MUGHAL CHICKEN BIRYANI 180
(Rice with Cinnamon and Almonds)

FISH BIRYANI 181
(Rice with Fish and Coconut Milk)

SINDHI BIRYANI 182
(Rice with Spicy Lamb and Dates)

KOLKATA BIRYANI 184
(Rice with Lamb, Rosewater and Saffron)

SRI LANKAN SHRIMP BIRYANI 187
(Rice with Spicy Green Chile)

VEGETABLE PANEER
BIRYANI

VEG **GF** (RICE WITH VEGETABLES AND CHEESE)

This is a decidedly casual biryani; I think of it as almost the Indian version of a simple vegetable stir-fry. Part of what makes it easy is its flexibility—feel free to swap in spinach, broccoli or any other vegetable loitering around your crisper drawer. I like to use Cilantro Chile Paneer in this biryani, but any kind of firm paneer will work.

2   cups (500 mL) **white basmati rice**

2   cups (500 mL) **water**

3   tablespoons (45 mL) **ghee**

1   large **onion**, chopped

1   tablespoon (15 mL) minced **ginger**

1   tablespoon (15 mL) minced **garlic**

6   **green cardamom pods**, cracked (see page 21)

2   teaspoons (10 mL) freshly ground **black pepper**

1   teaspoon (5 mL) **cumin seeds**

1   teaspoon (5 mL) ground **turmeric**

1   teaspoon (5 mL) **Kashmiri chili powder**

1   teaspoon (5 mL) **Garam Masala** (page 24) or store-bought

1   tablespoon (15 mL) **kosher salt**

1   cup (250 mL) thinly sliced **carrots**

1   **zucchini**, chopped

1   **red bell pepper**, chopped

14   ounces (420 g) **Cilantro Chile Paneer** (page 70) or store-bought **paneer**, cut into ½-inch (1 cm) cubes

2   cups (500 mL) boiling **water**

½   cup (125 mL) **Coconut Cilantro Chutney** (page 92) or store-bought

½   cup (125 mL) chopped fresh **cilantro**

1   Place the rice in a medium bowl and cover with 2 cups (500 mL) water. Let stand for 20 minutes, then drain and rinse.

2   Using the Sauté function on High, heat the ghee in the inner pot for 1 minute, until shimmering. Add the onion; cook, stirring occasionally, for about 6 minutes, until lightly browned.

3   Stir in the ginger and garlic; cook for about 1 minute, until fragrant. Stir in the cardamom pods, black pepper, cumin seeds, turmeric, chili powder, garam masala and salt; cook for about 1 minute, until fragrant. Add the carrots, zucchini, bell pepper and paneer; stir to combine. Stir in the rice and the boiling water.

4   Secure the lid and cook on high pressure for 3 minutes.

5   Once the cooking is complete, let the pressure release naturally for 5 minutes, then quick-release the remaining pressure.

6   Remove the lid. Stir in the chutney and cilantro; serve.

NOTE *Biryani is said to have come from Persia and was brought to India by the Mughals. It's since become the national celebration dish of India.*

Hyderabadi (GF)
BIRYANI

(SPICY RICE WITH CHICKEN)

Hyderabadi biryani is famously spicy, like much of the food from the state where it originates: Andhra Pradesh, in southeastern India. I suggest you start with a single chile pepper and then add more if you want more heat (if so—respect). But have a little Cucumber Raita (page 56) ready on the side just in case your bravado got the best of you, to cool things off.

½ cup (125 mL) **Plain Yogurt** (page 40) or store-bought

4 teaspoons (20 mL) minced **garlic**, divided

2 teaspoons (10 mL) **Garam Masala** (page 24) or store-bought

1 teaspoon (5 mL) **kosher salt**

1 teaspoon (5 mL) freshly ground **black pepper**

1 pound (500 g) boneless, skinless **chicken thighs**, cut into 1-inch (2.5 cm) pieces

2 tablespoons (30 mL) **ghee** or **vegetable oil**

1 **onion**, sliced

2 tablespoons (30 mL) minced **ginger**

1 tablespoon (15 mL) **Curry Powder** (page 23) or store-bought

1 teaspoon (5 mL) ground **cumin**

8 fresh **curry leaves**, torn into pieces

1 **serrano chile**, minced

2 cups (500 mL) **water**

2 cups (500 mL) **white basmati rice**, rinsed

½ cup (125 mL) chopped fresh **cilantro**

1 Combine the yogurt, 1 tablespoon (15 mL) garlic, garam masala, salt and pepper in a large bowl; whisk until smooth. Add the chicken and stir to coat evenly. Cover and transfer to the refrigerator for at least 30 minutes or up to 8 hours.

2 Using the Sauté function on High, heat the ghee in the inner pot for about 1 minute, until shimmering. Add the onion; cook for 4 minutes, stirring occasionally, until softened. Stir in the ginger, curry powder, cumin, curry leaves, chile and remaining garlic; cook for about 1 minute, until fragrant. Add the chicken, discarding any excess marinade; cook, stirring often, for about 5 minutes, until browned on all sides.

3 Stir in the water, using a wooden spoon to scrape up any browned bits from the bottom of the pot. Stir in the rice. Secure the lid and cook on high pressure for 5 minutes.

4 Once the cooking is complete, let the pressure release naturally for 5 minutes, then quick-release the remaining pressure.

5 Remove the lid and fluff the biryani with a fork. Top with cilantro and serve.

NOTE
If you ever go to a big wedding in India, look for the cooking tent, where you'll find massive pots of biryani cooked over an open fire, tended for hours by biryani masters. It's an incredible sight.

Mughal Chicken
BIRYANI

GF (RICE WITH CINNAMON AND ALMONDS)

This is a Persian-style dish, closer to the original biryani. Loaded with the almonds, cinnamon and other warm spices that Mughal cooking is famous for, this is a biryani for a chilly winter night when you feel like a fire, a glass of wine and a plate of something comforting.

Food processor or blender

- 1 tablespoon (15 mL) **Garam Masala** (page 24) or store-bought
- 1 teaspoon (5 mL) ground **cloves**
- 1 tablespoon (15 mL) **kosher salt**, divided
- 1 pound (500 g) boneless, skinless **chicken thighs**, cut into 1-inch (2.5 cm) pieces
- 4 **garlic cloves**
- 1 1-inch (2.5 cm) piece **ginger**, thinly sliced
- 1 cup (250 mL) **almonds**, toasted and chopped, divided (see page 32)
- 1 tablespoon (15 mL) **ghee** or **vegetable oil**
- 2 **onions**, chopped
- 2 2-inch (5 cm) **cinnamon sticks**
- 6 **green cardamom pods**, cracked (see page 21)
- 1½ cups (375 mL) **white basmati rice**, rinsed
- 1½ cups (375 mL) **water**
- ¼ cup (60 mL) chopped fresh **mint**

1 Combine the garam masala, cloves and 1 teaspoon (5 mL) salt in a large bowl. Add the chicken and toss to coat evenly. Cover and transfer to the refrigerator for at least 30 minutes or up to 12 hours.

2 Place the garlic, ginger and ½ cup (125 mL) almonds in a food processor or blender; process into a smooth paste.

3 Using the Sauté function on High, heat the ghee in the inner pot for about 1 minute, until shimmering. Add the onions; cook for about 4 minutes, stirring occasionally, until softened. Stir in the garlic-almond paste, chicken, remaining 2 teaspoons (10 mL) salt, cinnamon sticks, cardamom pods, rice and water. Secure the lid and cook on high pressure for 5 minutes.

4 Once the cooking is complete, let the pressure release naturally for 10 minutes, then quick-release the remaining pressure.

5 Transfer the biryani to a serving platter and garnish with the mint and remaining almonds; serve.

PREP	SAUTÉ	MANUAL	RELEASE	TOTAL	SERVES
15 MIN	**7 MIN**	**3 MIN**	**NATURAL/ QUICK**	**45 MIN**	**6**

FISH BIRYANI

GF (RICE WITH FISH AND COCONUT MILK)

With its white fish fillets, delicate spices, plenty of cilantro and coconut milk, this light, creamy biryani from southwestern India stands apart from the rest. I like to eat this on a summer night paired with margaritas (because why not?).

1½ cups (375 mL) **white basmati rice**

Water

1 pound (500 g) skinless delicate **white fish fillets** (snapper, barramundi or sea bass)

1 **lemon**, halved

1 tablespoon (15 mL) **kosher salt**, divided

2 **garlic cloves**, minced

1 tablespoon (15 mL) **vegetable oil**

2 **onions**, chopped

2 teaspoons (10 mL) ground **turmeric**

1 tablespoon (15 mL) minced **ginger**

1 **green Thai chile**, minced

1 can (14 oz/398 mL) full-fat **coconut milk**

1 cup (250 mL) chopped fresh **cilantro**, divided

1 Place the rice in a medium bowl and cover with 2 cups (500 mL) water. Let it stand for 20 minutes, then drain and rinse.

2 Place the fish in a shallow dish. Squeeze the lemon overtop and season with 1 teaspoon (5 mL) salt and the garlic, turning the fish to coat both sides.

3 Using the Sauté function on High, heat the oil in the inner pot for about 1 minute, until shimmering. Add the onions; cook for about 4 minutes, stirring occasionally, until softened. Stir in the turmeric, ginger and chile; cook for about 1 minute, until fragrant.

4 Add 1 cup (250 mL) water, stirring with a wooden spoon to scrape up any browned bits on the bottom of the pot. Stir in the rice, the remaining 2 teaspoons (10 mL) salt and coconut milk. Place the fish on top of the rice, then spoon some rice over the fish. Secure the lid and cook on high pressure for 3 minutes.

5 Once the cooking is complete, let the pressure release naturally for 5 minutes, then quick-release the remaining pressure.

6 Remove the lid; stir in ½ cup (125 mL) cilantro. Transfer to a platter, garnish with the remaining cilantro and serve.

Sindhi BIRYANI

GF (RICE WITH SPICY LAMB AND DATES)

The Sindhi people originally came from northwest India, which became part of Pakistan in the 1947 partition. Many of them moved south in order to stay in India, where they continue to celebrate their culture through dishes like this biryani. Since many Sindhis are also Muslims, lamb is used in this dish, while saffron, dates and almonds highlight the Persian influence of the Mughal Empire. This dish is rich and full of flavor; it's really nice for a special-occasion dinner.

½ cup (125 mL) **Plain Yogurt** (page 40) or store-bought

1 tablespoon (15 mL) minced **ginger**

2 tablespoons (30 mL) minced **garlic**, divided

2 tablespoons (30 mL) **ghee** or **vegetable oil**

1 teaspoon (5 mL) **Kashmiri chili powder**

1 teaspoon (5 mL) ground **turmeric**

3 teaspoons (15 mL) **kosher salt**, divided

2 teaspoons (10 mL) freshly ground **black pepper**, divided

1 pound (500 g) trimmed boneless **lamb shoulder**, cut into 1-inch (2.5 cm) pieces

2 tablespoons (30 mL) **vegetable oil**

2 **onions**, thinly sliced and divided

1 teaspoon (5 mL) ground **cloves**

8 **green cardamom pods**, cracked

1 teaspoon (5 mL) **cumin seeds**

1 2-inch (5 cm) **cinnamon stick**

1 **bay leaf**

2 cups (500 mL) **water**

10 **dates** or **prunes**, chopped

2 **serrano chiles**, finely chopped

2 medium **yellow-fleshed potatoes**, cut into chunks

1½ cups (375 mL) **brown basmati rice**, rinsed

1 teaspoon (5 mL) **saffron**

1 tablespoon (15 mL) chopped fresh **mint**

1 Whisk together the yogurt, ginger, 1 tablespoon (15 mL) garlic, ghee, chili powder, turmeric, 2 teaspoons (10 mL) salt and 1 teaspoon (5 mL) pepper in a large bowl. Add the lamb and stir to coat it evenly. Cover and transfer to the refrigerator for at least 30 minutes or up to 12 hours.

2 Using the Sauté function on High, heat the oil in the inner pot for about 1 minute, until shimmering. Add half the onions; cook, stirring occasionally, for about 10 minutes, until evenly browned. Transfer to a small bowl.

3 Place the remaining onion, cloves, cardamom pods, remaining 1 teaspoon (5 mL) pepper, cumin seeds, cinnamon stick, bay leaf and remaining 1 tablespoon (15 mL) garlic in the inner pot; stir to combine and cook for 1 minute, until fragrant. Add the remaining 1 teaspoon (5 mL) salt and water, using a wooden spoon to scrape up any browned bits on the bottom of the pot. Add the dates, chiles, potatoes, lamb and yogurt marinade, rice and saffron; stir to combine.

4 Secure the lid and cook on high pressure for 23 minutes.

5 Once the cooking is complete, let the pressure release naturally for 5 minutes, then quick-release the remaining pressure.

6 Remove the lid and stir. Transfer to a serving platter and top with reserved browned onions and mint; serve.

NOTE *When you cook the meat and rice together like this, it infuses all the spices and aromatics into the rice. This is the* kacchi *method of making biryani—in which marinated uncooked meat is layered with uncooked rice and then cooked together slowly—and it just so happens to be perfect for the Instant Pot.*

KOLKATA BIRYANI

 (RICE WITH LAMB, ROSEWATER AND SAFFRON)

This biryani, from Kolkata in West Bengal, features potatoes infused with rosewater and saffron, along with lamb or goat. The rosewater, star anise and saffron give this biryani floral notes that provide a gorgeous contrast to the richness of the lamb. You'll need to do pot-in-pot cooking to prepare everything at once for this biryani—this simply means we're going to stack things up and cook them separately, but together and at the same time.

Instant Pot trivet

- 1 teaspoon (5 mL) ground **cardamom**
- 1 teaspoon (5 mL) ground **cumin**
- 1 teaspoon (5 mL) ground **coriander**
- 1 teaspoon (5 mL) freshly ground **black pepper**
- 1 tablespoon (15 mL) **kosher salt**, divided (approx.)
  Pinch ground **nutmeg**
  Pinch ground **cloves**

- ½ cup (125 mL) **Plain Yogurt** (page 40) or store-bought
- 1 pound (500 g) trimmed boneless **lamb stewing meat**, cut into 1-inch (2.5 cm) pieces
- 1 cup (250 mL) **water**, divided
- 2 teaspoons (10 mL) **saffron**
- 1 teaspoon (5 mL) **rosewater**
- ½ pound (250 g) **yellow-fleshed potatoes**, chopped into 1-inch (2.5 cm) pieces
- 2 tablespoons (30 mL) **ghee**
- 2 **onions**, chopped
- 1 tablespoon (15 mL) **Garam Masala** (page 24) or store-bought
- 1 **star anise pod**
- 2 2-inch (5 cm) **cinnamon sticks**
- 1½ cups (375 mL) **white basmati rice**, rinsed
- ½ cup (125 mL) chopped **mint**

1 Combine the cardamom, cumin, coriander, pepper, 1 teaspoon (5 mL) salt, nutmeg and cloves in a large bowl. Whisk in the yogurt. Add the lamb and stir to coat evenly. Cover and transfer to the refrigerator for at least 1 hour or up to 12 hours.

2 Place the lamb, marinade and ½ cup (125 mL) water in the inner pot; stir. Place the Instant Pot trivet on top of the lamb.

3 Pour ½ cup (125 mL) water in an insert pan or ovenproof bowl. Stir the saffron, rosewater and a pinch of salt into the water in the insert pan, then add the potatoes. Place the insert pan on top of the trivet. Secure the lid and cook on high pressure for 7 minutes.

4 Once the cooking is complete, quick-release the pressure.

5 Remove the trivet and the insert pan containing the potatoes. Transfer the lamb and accumulated juices to a large bowl.

6 Using the Sauté function on High, heat the ghee in the inner pot for about 1 minute, until shimmering. Add the onions and cook, stirring occasionally, for about 4 minutes, until softened. Stir in the remaining 2 teaspoons (10 mL) salt and garam masala; cook for about 1 minute, until fragrant.

7 Return the lamb and accumulated juices to the inner pot. Add the star anise pod and cinnamon sticks. Stir in the rice and the reserved cooking water from the potatoes. Secure the lid and cook on high pressure for 5 minutes.

8 Once the cooking is complete, release the pressure naturally for 10 minutes, then quick-release the remaining pressure.

9 Remove the lid. Chop the potatoes and stir them into the biryani. Garnish with mint; serve.

NOTE *You can use a metal pressure cooker insert pan or any ovenproof glass or ceramic bowl to cook the potatoes.*

Sri Lankan SHRIMP GF BIRYANI

(RICE WITH SPICY GREEN CHILE)

I love this biryani for a couple of reasons. First, the combo of shrimp, lime juice, turmeric and smoked paprika is so sunny and bright it's positively beachy. Second, this is the fastest biryani you can make (hello, Tuesday-night dinner!). Using very hot water in the dish means the Instant Pot will build up pressure quickly, so you won't overcook the shrimp.

2 cups (500 mL) **white basmati rice**

2 cups (500 mL) **water**

2 teaspoons (10 mL) **vegetable oil**

1 **onion**, chopped

1 **serrano chile**, minced

2 tablespoons (30 mL) minced **ginger**

1 tablespoon (15 mL) minced **garlic**

1 teaspoon (5 mL) **Kashmiri chili powder**

1 teaspoon (5 mL) ground **turmeric**

1 teaspoon (5 mL) **smoked paprika**

2 teaspoons (10 mL) **kosher salt**

10 fresh **curry leaves,** torn into pieces

1½ cups (375 mL) **boiling water**

1½ pounds (750 g) raw **shrimp** (size 16/20 or larger; see Note), thawed if frozen, peeled and deveined

1 can (15 oz/425 mL) diced **tomatoes** (with juice)

2 teaspoons (10 mL) freshly squeezed **lime juice**

½ cup (125 mL) minced fresh **cilantro**

1   Place the rice in a bowl and cover with 2 cups (500 mL) water. Let stand for 20 minutes, then drain and rinse.

2   Using the Sauté function on High, heat the oil in the inner pot for about 1 minute, until shimmering. Add the onion; cook for about 4 minutes, until softened. Stir in the chile, ginger, garlic, chili powder, turmeric, paprika, salt and curry leaves; cook for about 1 minute, until fragrant. Stir in the boiling water; using a wooden spoon, stir, scraping up any browned bits on the bottom of the pot. Stir in the rice, shrimp and tomatoes (with juice).

3   Secure the lid and cook on high pressure for 3 minutes.

4   Once the cooking is complete, quick-release the pressure.

5   Remove the lid and stir in the lime juice. Transfer to a platter, garnish with cilantro and serve.

NOTE   *Make sure to use jumbo shrimp or larger for this recipe, since smaller shrimp will be overcooked by the time the rice is finished. Look for "16/20" or "U/15" on the package; this indicates how many shrimps there are per pound.*

Lentils
CHICKPEAS
and
PULSES

DAL *Makhani*

VEG GF (CREAMY SPICED LENTILS)

Ancient lentil legends (it's a thing) declare that dal makhani takes exactly 142 minutes and 47 stirs to make. Having that much time to focus on one thing seems like an immersive art experiment to me—maybe I'll try it in another lifetime. But I can't wait that long to make this buttery, creamy lentil stew. Here's a much faster version that doesn't require soaking the lentils in advance.

2	teaspoons (10 mL) **ghee** or **vegetable oil**
1	**onion**, chopped
2	teaspoons (10 mL) minced **ginger**
1	teaspoon (5 mL) ground **cumin**
2	teaspoons (10 mL) **kosher salt** (approx.)
1	teaspoon (5 mL) **Kashmiri chili powder**
½	teaspoon (2 mL) **Garam Masala** (page 24) or store-bought
1	tablespoon (15 mL) minced **garlic**
1	can (14 oz/398 mL) diced **tomatoes** (with juice)
1	cup (250 mL) dried whole **black urad dal** or **beluga lentils**, rinsed
½	cup (125 mL) dried **kidney beans**, rinsed (optional)
2	**bay leaves**
3½	cups (875 mL) **water**
¼	cup (60 mL) **heavy** or **whipping** (35%) **cream**
½	cup (125 mL) chopped fresh **cilantro**

1 Using the Sauté function on High, heat the ghee in the inner pot for 1 minute, until shimmering. Add the onion, ginger, cumin, salt, chili powder and garam masala; cook, stirring frequently, for 1 minute, until the spices are fragrant. Stir in the garlic; cook for 1 minute, stirring frequently, until fragrant.

2 Add the tomatoes (with juice); cook, stirring, for 1 minute, until well combined.

3 Add the dal, kidney beans (if using), bay leaves and water. Secure the lid and cook on high pressure for 30 minutes.

4 Once the cooking is complete, let the pressure release naturally.

5 Remove the lid and, using the back of a spoon, gently mash about half the dal (more or less, depending on your preferred mush level). Stir in the cream, taste and add more salt if needed. Transfer to a platter, garnish with cilantro and serve.

LENTIL

VEG **GF** SALAD

WITH PANEER AND TOMATOES

This is sort of like a dal turned into a light salad, making it an easy chilled or room-temperature lunch or dinner on a warm day. I like using Firm Paneer, Cilantro Chile Paneer (page 70) or Coriander Black Pepper Paneer (page 69) in this recipe, but any kind will do. If you'd like to add some crunch, sauté the paneer cubes in hot oil until they are golden brown—it turns them into the cheese croutons we all deserve.

- 2 tablespoons (30 mL) **vegetable oil**
- 1 **onion**, chopped
- 2 teaspoons (10 mL) **Garam Masala** (page 24) or store-bought
- 1 teaspoon (5 mL) ground **cumin**
- 1 teaspoon (5 mL) ground **coriander**
- 1 teaspoon (5 mL) **kosher salt** (approx.)
- ½ teaspoon (2 mL) **amchur powder**
- 2 teaspoons (10 mL) minced **garlic**
- 2 **carrots**, chopped
- 2 cups (500 mL) low-sodium **vegetable broth**
- 1 cup (250 mL) dried whole **black urad dal** or **beluga lentils**, rinsed
- 1 tablespoon (15 mL) **olive oil**
- 1 cup (250 mL) cubed **Firm Paneer** (page 68) or store-bought
- 2 **tomatoes**, chopped
- 2 tablespoons (30 mL) chopped fresh **mint** or **basil**

1 Using the Sauté function on High, heat the vegetable oil in the inner pot for 1 minute, until shimmering. Add the onion; cook, stirring occasionally, for about 4 minutes, until softened. Stir in the garam masala, cumin, coriander, salt and amchur; cook for about 1 minute, until fragrant.

2 Stir in the garlic and carrots; cook for about 1 minute, until the garlic is fragrant. Add the vegetable broth and stir, using a wooden spoon to scrape up any browned bits on the bottom of the pot. Stir in the lentils. Secure the lid and cook on high pressure for 9 minutes.

3 Once the cooking is complete, let the pressure release naturally for 5 minutes, then quick-release the remaining pressure.

4 Remove the lid. Stir in the olive oil, paneer, tomatoes and mint. Taste and add more salt if needed; serve at room temperature or chilled.

NOTE *I often add a giant dollop of Plain Yogurt (page 40) or raita on top of this salad.*

TOOR DAL

VEG · GF · V

(TANGY LENTIL STEW WITH PEANUTS)

I love the combination of tangy flavor from the kokum or tamarind and the sweetness from the jaggery. Seek out toor dal—a.k.a. pigeon peas or yellow lentils—for this dal, which comes from Gujarat. This seems incredibly basic until you spoon the toasted curry leaves and peanuts overtop and suddenly, you're eating dinner enhanced by the world's greatest party mix.

- 2 cups (500 mL) dried **toor dal**, rinsed
- 1 tablespoon (15 mL) **kosher salt**
- 1 tablespoon (15 mL) **jaggery** or **brown sugar**
- 4 cups (1 L) **water**
- 8 pieces dried **kokum** or ½ cup (125 mL) **tamarind paste**
- 3 tablespoons (45 mL) **vegetable oil** or **coconut oil**, divided
- 1 tablespoon (15 mL) minced **ginger**
- 2 teaspoons (10 mL) **mustard seeds**
- 2 teaspoons (10 mL) **cumin seeds**
- 2 teaspoons (10 mL) ground **turmeric**
- ½ cup (125 mL) salted **peanuts**
- 12 fresh **curry leaves**, torn into pieces

1 Place the toor dal, salt, jaggery, water and kokum in the inner pot. Secure the lid and cook on high pressure for 10 minutes.

2 Meanwhile, heat 2 tablespoons (30 mL) oil in a small skillet. Stir in the ginger; cook for about 1 minute, until softened. Add the mustard seeds, cumin seeds and turmeric; cook for about 2 minutes, stirring frequently, until fragrant. Remove the skillet from the heat.

3 Once the dal is cooked, let the pressure release naturally.

4 Remove the lid and remove the kokum from the pot; discard. Using a wooden spoon, mash about three-quarters of the lentils.

5 Stir the tempered spice mixture into the dal. Heat the remaining 1 tablespoon (15 mL) oil in the skillet. Add the peanuts and curry leaves; cook, tossing the pan regularly, for about 2 minutes, until the peanuts are toasted and the leaves are sizzling.

6 Transfer the dal to a platter, pour the peanut mixture overtop and serve.

NOTE *Kokum is a dark purple fruit grown in southern India. It is most often sold dried and is used to infuse a tart, sour flavor into soups and stews like this one. You can find it in Indian grocery stores or online.*

BENGALI CHOLAR DAL

VEG · GF · V **(COCONUT CHICKPEA STEW)**

Dal, coconut and puris (page 257) were the holy trinity of my meals when I was a kid, and this mild Bengali dal takes me right back to the parties my grandparents used to throw when we visited India. Dozens of family and friends would line up at tables in the courtyard behind the house, eating dal off banana leaves, while my cousins and I raced in and out, angling for a few bites before sneaking up to the roof to watch the fireworks. I still eat this with my hands, scooping it up with loads of puris, just like when I was a kid.

2 cups (500 mL) dried **chana dal**, rinsed

4 teaspoons (20 mL) **kosher salt**, divided

6 cups (1.5 L) **water**

2 teaspoons (10 mL) granulated **sugar** (see Note)

3 tablespoons (45 mL) freshly squeezed **lemon juice**

2 tablespoons (30 mL) **vegetable oil**

1 tablespoon (15 mL) minced **ginger**

½ cup (125 mL) unsweetened **coconut flakes**

1 cup (250 mL) **cashews**

½ cup (125 mL) **raisins**

1 teaspoon (5 mL) ground **turmeric**

1 teaspoon (5 mL) **Garam Masala** (page 24) or store-bought

1 teaspoon (5 mL) **Kashmiri chili powder**

Pinch **asafoetida** (optional)

1 Place the chana dal, 1 teaspoon (5 mL) salt and the water in the inner pot. Secure the lid and cook on high pressure for 15 minutes.

2 Once the cooking is complete, let the pressure release naturally. Check to make sure the chana dal is soft enough for your liking; if it is still too hard, cook it on high pressure for another 5 minutes.

3 Stir in the remaining 1 tablespoon (15 mL) salt, sugar and lemon juice. Using the Sauté function on Low, simmer for 5 minutes, stirring occasionally, until thickened.

4 While the dal is simmering, heat the oil in a small skillet over medium heat, until shimmering. Add the ginger and cook for 1 minute, until fragrant. Stir in the coconut, cashews, raisins, turmeric, garam masala, chili powder and asafoetida (if using); toast for about 2 minutes, stirring frequently, until fragrant.

5 Garnish the dal with the toasted cashew-spice tempering and serve.

NOTE *Bone char is often used to process sugar, so if you're eating vegan, make sure to buy organic sugar, which hasn't been filtered this way. If you don't follow a vegan diet, you can use regular granulated sugar.*

RAJASTHANI PANCHMEL DAL

   (MIX OF FIVE DALS)

This dal is one the most popular dishes in Rajasthani cooking. *Panch* means five, so you are supposed to use five different dals here, but if you have only two or three, I promise not to call the dal police on you. The good news is that once you have all your dals collected, the dish comes together pretty quickly.

- 4 teaspoons (20 mL) **vegetable oil**, divided
- 1 **onion**, chopped
- 1 tablespoon (15 mL) minced **ginger**
- 4 **garlic cloves**, minced
- 2 teaspoons (10 mL) **kosher salt**
- Pinch **asafoetida**
- 2 **green Thai chiles**, minced
- 1 teaspoon (5 mL) ground **turmeric**
- 1 teaspoon (5 mL) ground **cinnamon**
- 1 can (14 oz/398 mL) diced **tomatoes** (with juice)
- 2½ cups (625 mL) **water**
- ⅓ cup (75 mL) dried **toor dal**, rinsed
- ⅓ cup (75 mL) dried **green moong dal**, rinsed
- ⅓ cup (75 mL) dried **red masoor dal**, rinsed
- ⅓ cup (75 mL) dried **chana dal**, rinsed
- ⅓ cup (75 mL) dried **yellow moong dal**, rinsed
- 1 teaspoon (5 mL) **brown** or **yellow mustard seeds**
- 1 teaspoon (5 mL) **cumin seeds**
- 1 **dried red chile**, broken into pieces
- ½ cup (125 mL) chopped fresh **cilantro**

1 Using the Sauté function on High, heat 2 teaspoons (10 mL) oil in the inner pot for about 1 minute, until shimmering. Add the onion; cook, stirring occasionally, for about 4 minutes, until softened. Stir in the ginger, garlic, salt and asafoetida; cook for about 2 minutes, until fragrant. Stir in the green chiles, turmeric and cinnamon; cook for 1 minute, until fragrant.

2 Add the tomatoes (with juice) and water; stir, using a wooden spoon to scrape up any browned bits on the bottom of the pot. Stir in the toor dal, green moong dal, masoor dal, chana dal and yellow moong dal. Secure the lid and cook on high pressure for 8 minutes.

3 Meanwhile, heat the remaining 2 teaspoons (10 mL) oil in a small skillet. Add the mustard seeds, cumin seeds and dried chile; cook for about 1 minute, until the mustard seeds begin to pop. Set aside.

4 Once the dal is cooked, let the pressure release naturally.

5 Remove the lid and stir the dal. Transfer to a bowl and pour the tempered spice mixture overtop. Garnish with cilantro and serve.

PREP	SAUTÉ	MANUAL	RELEASE	TOTAL	SERVES
10 MIN	17 MIN	35 MIN	NATURAL/ QUICK	1 HR 15 MIN	6

CHANA MASALA

VEG **GF** **V** (STEWED CHICKPEAS, TOMATOES AND ONIONS)

Can you live without eating chana masala on the regular? If so, I don't want to know. This Punjabi stew (also known as chole masala) is another of those classic Indian dishes everyone knows and loves. The tanginess you get from amchur powder is key here, but if you can't find it, lemon juice will work in a pinch. I add greens to my version for a little color and variety, and sometimes chop up some chicken to throw in there as well.

3 tablespoons (45 mL) **vegetable oil**, divided

1 **onion**, finely chopped

Water

2 teaspoons (10 mL) **yellow** or **black mustard seeds**

2 teaspoons (10 mL) ground **coriander**

2 teaspoons (10 mL) **Garam Masala** (page 24) or store-bought

1 teaspoon (5 mL) ground **cumin**

2 teaspoons (10 mL) **kosher salt** (approx.)

1 teaspoon (5 mL) ground **turmeric**

2 teaspoons (10 mL) **amchur powder** or freshly squeezed **lemon juice** (approx.)

2 tablespoons (30 mL) minced **garlic**

1 tablespoon (15 mL) minced **ginger**

1 **serrano chile**, minced

1 can (14 oz/398 mL) diced **tomatoes** (with juice)

2 cups (500 mL) dried **chickpeas**, rinsed (see Note)

2 cups (500 mL) chopped **greens** (spinach, beet greens or mustard greens)

2 teaspoons (10 mL) freshly squeezed **lemon juice** (optional)

1 cup (250 mL) finely chopped fresh **cilantro**

1   Using the Sauté function on High, heat 2 tablespoons (30 mL) oil in the inner pot for 1 minute, until shimmering. Add the onions; cook, stirring occasionally, for about 10 minutes, occasionally adding 1 tablespoon (15 mL) water if the bottom of the pot gets brown and the onion begins to stick. Cook the onion until deeply browned.

2   Push the onion to the side of the pot. Add the remaining 1 tablespoon (15 mL) oil and heat it for 1 minute, until shimmering. Stir in the mustard seeds, coriander, garam masala, cumin, salt and turmeric; cook for about 1 minute, until the mustard seeds begin to pop. Stir in the amchur, garlic, ginger and chile; cook for 1 minute, until fragrant.

3   Add the diced tomatoes (with juice) and 2 cups (500 mL) water; stir, using a wooden spoon to scrape up any browned bits on the bottom of the pot. Stir in the chickpeas. Secure the lid and cook on high pressure for 35 minutes.

4   Once the cooking is complete, release the pressure naturally for 5 minutes, then quick-release the remaining pressure. Check to make sure the chickpeas are soft enough for your liking; if they are still too hard, cook them on high pressure for another 5 minutes.

5   Remove the lid and stir in the chopped greens, adding a little more water if the stew is dry. Using the Sauté setting on High, simmer until the greens are wilted, about 2 minutes. Taste and add more salt and lemon juice, if needed. Stir in the cilantro and serve.

NOTE *I sometimes cook extra chickpeas on the weekend so I can throw this dish together on a weeknight in just a few minutes. If you have cooked chickpeas on hand, you can modify this recipe by using 6 cups (1.5 L) cooked chickpeas and only ½ cup (125 mL) water. Decrease the cooking time in Step 3 to 5 minutes.*

PREP	MANUAL	RELEASE	TOTAL	SERVES
10 MIN	**11 MIN**	**NATURAL/ QUICK**	**40 MIN**	**4**

APPLE POMEGRANATE MOONG DAL BOWL

VEG **GF** **V**

I love a light vegetable bowl for lunch, especially this one, which has loads of fresh, bright flavors from the apples, celery and pomegranate, not to mention the lemon-fennel dressing. Don't worry if you can't find pomegranate seeds; this salad is still tart and refreshing without them.

1½ cups (375 mL) dried whole **green moong beans**, rinsed

4 cups (1 L) **water**

1 teaspoon (5 mL) **fennel seeds**

1 teaspoon (5 mL) ground **coriander**

1 teaspoon (5 mL) ground **cumin**

1 teaspoon (5 mL) **Chaat Masala** (page 25) or store-bought

1 teaspoon (5 mL) **kosher salt**

½ teaspoon (2 mL) freshly ground **black pepper**

2 tablespoons (30 mL) freshly squeezed **lemon juice**

2 tablespoons (30 mL) **olive oil**

1 large **apple**, chopped

2 **celery stalks**, chopped

1 cup (250 mL) **pomegranate seeds**

¼ cup (60 mL) chopped fresh **cilantro**

1   Place the moong beans and water in the inner pot. Cook on high pressure for 11 minutes.

2   Once the cooking is complete, let the pressure release naturally for 5 minutes, then quick-release the remaining pressure. Drain the beans.

3   Combine the fennel seeds, coriander, cumin, chaat masala, salt and pepper in a large bowl. Whisk in the lemon juice and oil.

4   Add the moong beans to the dressing and toss to coat. Add the apple, celery and pomegranate seeds; toss to combine. Stir in the cilantro and serve.

COCONUT CHILE
SUMMER VEGETABLE
VEG GF V
KOOTU

(STEWED VEGETABLES AND MOONG BEANS)

Anyone with access to zucchini from a garden, farmers' market or grocery store will appreciate this way to use up their summer produce haul in an all-American take on a south Indian dish from Tamil Nadu. The corn adds a nice sweetness and textural contrast to the moong beans, while the zucchini simply relaxes and melts into the spices. Is there anything more summery than that?

3 tablespoons (45 mL) **vegetable oil**

1 large **onion**, chopped

1 **serrano chile**, minced

1 tablespoon (15 mL) minced **garlic**

1 tablespoon (15 mL) minced **ginger**

1 teaspoon (5 mL) **brown** or **yellow mustard seeds**

2 teaspoons (10 mL) **Curry Powder** (page 23) or store-bought

10 fresh **curry leaves**, torn into pieces

2 teaspoons (10 mL) **kosher salt** (approx.)

Pinch **asafoetida**

1 cup **water** (250 mL)

1 cup (250 mL) **corn** kernels, fresh or thawed, if frozen

1 medium **zucchini**, chopped

1 cup (250 mL) dried **moong beans**, rinsed

¼ cup (60 mL) unsweetened **coconut flakes**

1 cup (250 mL) full-fat **coconut milk**

½ cup (125 mL) chopped fresh **herbs** (cilantro, dill, basil and/or parsley)

1 Using the Sauté function on High, heat the oil in the inner pot for about 1 minute, until shimmering. Add the onion, chile, garlic and ginger; cook for 1 minute, until fragrant. Add the mustard seeds, curry powder, curry leaves, salt and asafoetida; cook for about 2 minutes, until the mustard seeds begin to pop.

2 Stir in the water, corn, zucchini, moong beans and coconut. Secure the lid and cook on high pressure for 12 minutes.

3 Once the cooking is complete, let the pressure release naturally for 5 minutes, then quick-release the remaining pressure.

4 Remove the lid and stir in the coconut milk and herbs. Taste and add more salt, if needed. Serve.

Meat

AND

SEAFOOD

BUTTER CHICKEN

GF WITH SPICED CASHEWS

I used to feel pretty conflicted about butter chicken. It's pretty decadently delicious, but it's so often poorly cooked and then doused with way too much cream to compensate. I changed my tune while writing this book, since almost every friend who came to dinner while I was testing recipes asked/dropped hints/begged for butter chicken. I cut down the amount of cream, so it isn't as heavy, and added some—not traditional but highly recommended—puréed chipotle chiles in adobo sauce for a deeper, more complex, smokier flavor.

- 2 tablespoons (30 mL) **ghee** or **vegetable oil**
- 2 cups (500 mL) finely diced **onions**
- 1 teaspoon (5 mL) **kosher salt**
- 1 tablespoon (15 mL) minced **ginger**
- 1 tablespoon (15 mL) minced **garlic**
- ½ teaspoon (2 mL) ground **turmeric**
- 3 teaspoons (15 mL) **Kashmiri chili powder**, divided
- 1 teaspoon (5 mL) **Garam Masala** (page 24) or store-bought
- 2 tablespoons (30 mL) **tomato paste**
- 2 tablespoons (30 mL) **chipotle chiles in adobo sauce**, puréed or finely chopped
- 1 cup (250 mL) **water**
- 1 can (14 oz/398 mL) diced **tomatoes** (with juice)
- 2 pounds (1 kg) boneless, skinless **chicken thighs**, cut into 2-inch (5 cm) pieces
- ½ cup (125 mL) raw **cashew pieces**
- ¾ cup (175 mL) **heavy** or **whipping** (35%) **cream**
- ½ cup (125 mL) chopped fresh **cilantro**, divided

1 Using the Sauté function on High, heat the ghee in the inner pot for about 1 minute, until shimmering. Add the onions and salt; cook, stirring occasionally, for about 4 minutes, until the onions are softened. Add the ginger, garlic, turmeric, 2 teaspoons (10 mL) chili powder, garam masala and tomato paste; cook, stirring constantly, for about 1 minute, until fragrant. Stir in the chipotles in adobo sauce, water, tomatoes (with juice) and chicken.

2 Secure the lid and cook on high pressure for 8 minutes.

3 Meanwhile, toast the cashews in a small, dry skillet over medium heat, for 3 minutes, tossing the pan frequently, until lightly browned. Transfer to a medium bowl. Add the remaining 1 teaspoon (5 mL) chili powder and toss to coat. Set aside.

4 Once the chicken is cooked, let the pressure release naturally for 10 minutes, then quick-release the remaining pressure.

5 Remove the lid. If the sauce is watery, use the Sauté function on High to simmer the mixture for 5 minutes, until the sauce is reduced to the desired consistency. Stir in the cream and ¼ cup (60 mL) cilantro. Transfer the chicken and sauce to a serving dish, garnish with the remaining cilantro and cashews and serve.

NOTE *You can make this vegetarian by using paneer instead of chicken and make it vegan by substituting firm tofu for the chicken and coconut milk for the heavy cream.*

KERALA CHICKEN CURRY

 (CHICKEN WITH COCONUT MILK)

Kerala is a big tourist-beach destination, but it's also where many of the spices that India is known for are grown. You can taste them in this rich curry, which is loaded with the warm flavors of cinnamon, chiles and cloves. I make sure to serve this one over plenty of rice to soak up the sauce; Coconut Cilantro Rice Pilaf (page 162) works particularly well.

Coffee/spice grinder

1	teaspoon (5 mL) **Kashmiri chili powder**
½	teaspoon (2 mL) ground **turmeric**
1	teaspoon (5 mL) **Garam Masala** (page 24) or store-bought
¼	teaspoon (1 mL) freshly ground **black pepper**
2	teaspoons (10 mL) **kosher salt** (approx.)
2	tablespoons (30 mL) freshly squeezed **lemon juice**

2	pounds (1 kg) boneless, skinless **chicken thighs**, cut into 2-inch (5 cm) pieces
1½	tablespoons (22 mL) **coriander seeds**
1	2-inch (5 cm) **cinnamon stick**
4	whole **cloves**
2	**green cardamom pods**
1	teaspoon (5 mL) **fennel seeds**
¼	teaspoon (1 mL) ground **cumin**
¼	teaspoon (1 mL) **black peppercorns**
4	**dried red chiles**, divided
3	tablespoons (45 mL) **ghee** or **coconut oil**, divided
1	**onion**, sliced
1	teaspoon (5 mL) minced **ginger**
2	teaspoons (10 mL) minced **garlic**
1	can (14 oz/398 mL) full-fat **coconut milk**
12	fresh **curry leaves**, torn into pieces

1   Combine the chili powder, turmeric, garam masala and black pepper in a small skillet over medium heat. Toast for about 2 minutes, shaking occasionally, until fragrant. Transfer the toasted spice mixture to a large bowl. Set aside the skillet.

2   Add the salt and lemon juice to the spice mixture and stir to combine. Rub the marinade all over the chicken until evenly coated. Cover the chicken and refrigerate for at least 30 minutes or up to 8 hours.

3   Place the coriander seeds, cinnamon stick, cloves, cardamom pods, fennel seeds, cumin, peppercorns and 2 dried chiles in the reserved skillet. Toast over medium heat for about 2 minutes, shaking the pan occasionally, until fragrant. Remove the skillet from the heat. When the spices are cool enough to handle, break the chiles into pieces and crack open the cardamom pods, retrieving the seeds and discarding the pods. Transfer the toasted spices to a clean coffee/ spice grinder and grind to a powder. Set aside the skillet.

4   Using the Sauté function on High, heat 2 tablespoons (30 mL) ghee in the inner pot for about 1 minute, until shimmering. Add the onion; cook, stirring occasionally, for about 4 minutes, until softened. Stir in the ginger, garlic and ground toasted spices; cook for 1 minute, until fragrant.

5   Add the coconut milk and, using a wooden spoon, stir, scraping up any browned bits on the bottom of the pot. Stir in the chicken. Secure the lid and cook on high pressure for 6 minutes.

6   Once the cooking is complete, let the pressure release naturally for 10 minutes, then quick-release the remaining pressure.

7   Remove the lid and stir the curry. Taste and add additional salt, if needed. Using the Sauté function on Low, simmer for 5 minutes, until the sauce thickens slightly.

8   While the curry simmers, return the skillet to medium heat; add the remaining 1 tablespoon (15 mL) ghee and heat for about 1 minute, until shimmering. Tear the remaining dried chiles into pieces; add them to the pan along with the curry leaves. Cook for about 1 minute, until the curry leaves are sizzling. Pour the tempered spice mixture over the curry and serve.

CASHEW CHICKEN
KORMA

GF **(CHICKEN WITH CASHEW YOGURT SAUCE)**

This is a perfect gateway curry for people who are afraid of Indian food because they think it's always spicy-hot. This dish features warm (but not hot!) spices and a creamy sauce made from cashews and yogurt—you'll want to serve it with rice so you can enjoy every drop of the sauce. If you can't find cashews (or are anti-cashew for some reason), use blanched almonds instead.

High-powered blender

- ½ cup (125 mL) raw **cashews**
- 1 cup (250 mL) **water**
- 1 cup (250 mL) **Plain Yogurt** (page 40) or store-bought
- 4 teaspoons (20 mL) **kosher salt**, divided
- 1 teaspoon (5 mL) **Garam Masala** (page 24) or store-bought
- ½ teaspoon (2 mL) **Kashmiri chili powder**
- ½ teaspoon (2 mL) ground **cloves**
- 2 pounds (1 kg) boneless, skinless **chicken thighs**, cut into 2-inch (5 cm) pieces
- 4 tablespoons (60 mL) **ghee** or **vegetable oil**, divided
- 2 2-inch (5 cm) **cinnamon sticks**
- 8 **green cardamom pods**, cracked open
- 3 **onions**, thinly sliced
- ¼ cup (60 mL) minced **ginger**
- ¼ cup (60 mL) minced **garlic**
- 1 tablespoon (15 mL) freshly ground **black pepper**

- 1 teaspoon (5 mL) ground **turmeric**
- ¼ cup (60 mL) **heavy** or **whipping** (35%) **cream**
- 1 teaspoon (5 mL) **rosewater** (optional)
- ½ cup (125 mL) golden **raisins**
- ½ cup (125 mL) toasted **cashews** (see page 32)

1 Place the raw cashews in a bowl and cover with water. Soak for 2 hours.

2 Place the yogurt, 2 teaspoons (10 mL) salt, garam masala, chili powder and cloves in a large bowl; whisk until combined. Add the chicken and toss until evenly coated. Cover and refrigerate for at least 1 hour or up to 8 hours.

3 Using the Sauté function on High, heat 2 tablespoons (30 mL) ghee in the inner pot for 1 minute, until shimmering. Add the cinnamon sticks and cardamom pods; cook for about 1 minute, until fragrant.

4 Add the onions and the remaining 2 tablespoons (30 mL) ghee; cook, stirring occasionally, for about 5 to 7 minutes, until the onions are lightly browned.

5 Meanwhile, place the cashews and their soaking water in a high-powered blender. Blend on high speed into a smooth paste.

6   Stir in the ginger, garlic, pepper and turmeric to the onions; cook for about 1 minute, until fragrant. Stir in the cashew paste and the remaining 2 teaspoons (10 mL) salt; cook, stirring frequently, for about 1 minute, until the paste and onions are well combined. Stir in the chicken and marinade. Secure the lid and cook on high pressure for 8 minutes.

7   Once the cooking is complete, let the pressure release naturally for 10 minutes, then quick-release the remaining pressure.

8   Remove the lid and stir in the cream, rosewater (if using) and raisins. Using the Sauté function on Low, simmer for 2 minutes. Garnish with the toasted cashews and serve.

PREP	SAUTÉ	MANUAL	RELEASE	TOTAL	SERVES
15 MIN	**18 MIN**	**6 MIN**	**NATURAL/ QUICK**	**50 MIN**	**6**

CHICKEN JALFREZI
FRANKIES

(CHICKEN AND VEGETABLE WRAPS)

Depending on your perspective, frankies may seem like the tacos, burritos or gyros of India, but they are actually Indian-Chinese. The last time I was in Bombay (it's now called Mumbai, but I never remember to call it that) was when my brother Ravi lived there. He explained that there are more Chinese restaurants in Bombay than Indian restaurants, which kind of blew my mind until I learned there is a huge Chinese population in that part of India. Bombay Chinese food is a delicious mix of Chinese and Indian, and these chicken frankies are one of the most popular dishes from that hybrid cuisine.

4   teaspoons (20 mL) ground **coriander**, divided

4   teaspoons (20 mL) ground **cumin**, divided

4   teaspoons (20 mL) ground **turmeric**, divided

2   pounds (1 kg) boneless, skinless **chicken thighs**, cut into thin strips

2   tablespoons (30 mL) **vegetable oil**

1   large **onion**, sliced

2   teaspoons (10 mL) **Garam Masala** (page 24) or store-bought

1   **serrano chile**, minced

2   **garlic cloves**, minced

1   **red bell pepper**, chopped

½   cup (125 mL) **water**

1   can (14 oz/398 mL) diced **tomatoes** (with juice)

¼   cup (60 mL) chopped fresh **cilantro**

6   large pieces **Naan** (page 252) **Rotis** (page 256) or **tortillas**

1   cup (250 mL) **Cucumber Raita** (page 56) or store-bought

1   Combine 1 teaspoon (5 mL) coriander, 1 teaspoon (5 mL) cumin and 1 teaspoon (5 mL) turmeric in a large bowl. Add the chicken and toss until evenly coated.

2   Using the Sauté function on High, heat 1 tablespoon (15 mL) oil in the inner pot for about 1 minute, until shimmering. Add the chicken in 3 batches; cook each batch for 4 minutes, until browned on all sides, adding the remaining oil as needed. Transfer the browned chicken to a plate. Set aside.

3   Add the onion, remaining 1 tablespoon (15 mL) coriander, 1 tablespoon (15 mL) cumin and 1 table-spoon (15 mL) turmeric, garam masala, chile, garlic and bell pepper; cook, stirring occasionally, for about 5 to 7 minutes, until the onions are browned.

4   Stir in the water, using a wooden spoon to scrape up any browned bits from the bottom of the pot. Stir in the tomatoes (with juice) and chicken. Secure the lid and cook on high pressure for 6 minutes.

5   Once the cooking is complete, let the pressure release naturally for 10 minutes, then quick-release the remaining pressure.

6   Remove the lid and stir in the cilantro. Wrap the chicken mixture in pieces of naan and serve with the raita alongside.

GF *Assam Duck* RISOTTO

If butter chicken is what gets people to try making Indian food in the Instant Pot, then this duck risotto is what will keep them cooking. Yes, risotto is Italian, not Indian. But when you look at the food of Assam, which is in the far northwest of India, duck and rice are two of the most prevalent ingredients. They almost beg to be combined in a spiced risotto, which is so easy to make in an Instant Pot because you don't have to stir it.

1	tablespoon (15 mL) **Garam Masala** (page 24) or store-bought
4	teaspoons (20 mL) **kosher salt**, divided
2	bone-in **duck legs**, including thigh meat (about 8 oz/250 g)
1	**onion**, finely chopped
2	**garlic cloves**, minced
2	teaspoons (10 mL) minced **ginger**
2	cups (500 mL) **Arborio rice**
½	cup (125 mL) dry **white wine**
4	cups (1 L) low-sodium **chicken broth**

1 Combine the garam masala and 2 teaspoons (10 mL) salt in a large bowl. Add the duck and toss to coat completely in the mixture.

2 Using the Sauté function on High, heat the inner pot for 1 minute. Add the duck, skin side down, and cook for about 9 minutes, until the fat has started to render and the skin is brown and crisp. Flip the duck over and sear the other side for 5 minutes. Transfer to a plate and pour the rendered fat into a measuring cup.

3 Remove the skin from the duck. If it is not crunchy, return it to the inner pot and, using the Sauté function on High, cook, turning often, until crisp. Chop the skin and set it aside. Remove the meat from the legs and cut it into 1-inch (2.5 cm) pieces.

4 Using the Sauté function on High, heat 1 tablespoon (15 mL) rendered duck fat in the inner pot for about 1 minute, until hot. Add the onion and cook for 2 minutes, stirring occasionally, until beginning to soften. Then add the remaining 2 teaspoons (10 mL) salt, garlic and ginger; cook for about 1 minute, until fragrant. Stir in another tablespoon (15 mL) duck fat, the reserved duck meat and the rice. Add the wine and stir for about 1 minute, until combined. Stir in the chicken broth. Secure the lid and cook on high pressure for 7 minutes.

5 Once the cooking is complete, quick-release the pressure.

6 Remove the lid and stir. Simmer the risotto on the Keep Warm setting for 2 minutes, until it is thick and creamy. Taste and add more salt, if needed. Top the risotto with the crispy duck skin; serve.

VINDALOO

PULLED PORK PAV WITH TAMARIND BBQ SAUCE

I grew up in the American South, so grits, barbecue and biscuits are as much a part of my cooking as biryani. Needless to say, I love barbecued pulled pork sandwiches, so I created an Indian take on them, using vindaloo pork from Goa and serving it on a pav, which is an Indian slider bun. The tamarind barbecue sauce adds a nice tang that partners with the heat from the vindaloo pork, while the raita-ish slaw on top cools everything down.

PORK VINDALOO

- 1 tablespoon (15 mL) **kosher salt**
- 2 teaspoons (10 mL) **Garam Masala** (page 24) or store-bought
- 1 tablespoon (15 mL) **Kashmiri chili powder**
- 2 teaspoons (10 mL) **smoked paprika**
- 2 teaspoons (10 mL) ground **cumin**
- ¼ teaspoon (1 mL) ground **cloves**
- 3 pounds (1.5 kg) boneless **pork shoulder blade** (butt), cut into 1-inch (2.5 cm) pieces
- 4 tablespoons (60 mL) **vegetable oil**, divided
- ½ cup (125 mL) **water**
- 2 **onions**, finely chopped
- 1 teaspoon (5 mL) **brown mustard seeds**
- 2 tablespoons (30 mL) minced **ginger**
- 10 **garlic cloves**, minced
- ¼ cup (60 mL) **all-purpose flour**
- ½ cup (125 mL) **red wine vinegar**
- 1 2-inch (5 cm) **cinnamon stick**

TAMARIND BBQ SAUCE

- 1 tablespoon (15 mL) **vegetable oil**
- 2 teaspoons (10 mL) **cumin seeds**
- 1 teaspoon (5 mL) ground **ginger**
- 1 teaspoon (5 mL) ground **coriander**
- 1 teaspoon (5 mL) **cayenne pepper**
- ½ teaspoon (2 mL) **Garam Masala** (page 24) or store-bought
- 3 tablespoons (45 mL) **tamarind concentrate**
- ½ cup (125 mL) **brown sugar**
- 2 cups (500 mL) **water**

SERRANO LIME SLAW

- 1 cup (250 mL) **Plain Yogurt** (page 40) or store-bought
- ½ cup (125 mL) minced fresh **cilantro**
- ¼ cup (60 mL) minced fresh **mint**
- 1 **serrano chile**, halved lengthwise and very thinly sliced
- 2 tablespoons (30 mL) freshly squeezed **lime juice** Pinch **kosher salt**
- 1 cup (250 mL) shredded **green cabbage**
- 1 cup (250 mL) shredded **purple cabbage**
- ½ cup (125 mL) sliced **radishes**
- ¼ cup (60 mL) fresh **cilantro** leaves

SANDWICHES

- 18 **slider buns**, split

Recipe continues . . .

1 **PORK VINDALOO** Combine salt, garam masala, chili powder, paprika, cumin and cloves in a large bowl. Add the pork and rub the spices all over until evenly coated. Cover and refrigerate the meat for at least 30 minutes or up to 12 hours.

2 **TAMARIND BBQ SAUCE** Meanwhile, heat the oil in a medium saucepan over medium-high heat. Add the cumin seeds, ginger, coriander, cayenne pepper and garam masala. Cook for 2 minutes, stirring occasionally, until the spices are fragrant. Add the tamarind concentrate, brown sugar and water; cook, stirring constantly, for 1 minute, until the sugar dissolves. Reduce the heat to medium-low and simmer for 30 minutes, stirring occasionally, until the sauce is reduced by one-quarter and thickened (it should be thick enough to coat a spoon). Remove it from the heat.

3 **PORK VINDALOO** Using the Sauté function on High, heat 1 tablespoon (15 mL) oil in the inner pot for about 1 minute, until shimmering. Cook half of the pork for about 6 minutes, until browned on all sides; transfer the browned pork to a bowl. Repeat, using 1 tablespoon (15 mL) oil and the remaining pork. Add the water and, using a wooden spoon, stir, scraping up any browned bits on the bottom of the pot. Pour the liquid over the reserved pork.

4 Using the Sauté function on High, heat the remaining 2 tablespoons (30 mL) oil in the inner pot for about 1 minute, until shimmering. Add the onions and cook, stirring occasionally, for about 4 minutes, until softened. Stir in the mustard seeds, minced ginger and garlic; cook for about 1 minute, until the seeds begin to pop and the garlic is fragrant. Add the flour; cook, stirring constantly, for about 1 minute, until the onions are evenly coated. Add the vinegar and, using a wooden spoon, stir, scraping up any browned bits on the bottom of the pot. Stir in the pork, any accumulated juices and the cinnamon.

5 Secure the lid and cook on high pressure for 30 minutes.

6 **SERRANO LIME SLAW** Meanwhile, combine the yogurt, cilantro, mint, chile, lime juice and salt in a large bowl. Add the green cabbage, purple cabbage, radishes and cilantro. Toss to coat.

7 **PORK VINDALOO** Once the pork is cooked, let the pressure release naturally for 10 minutes, then quick-release the remaining pressure. Check the pork to make sure it's falling-apart tender; cook on high pressure for another 5 minutes if not. Season with salt to taste.

8 Let the pork rest until cool enough to handle. Remove the cinnamon stick, then shred the meat in the inner pot with two forks or your hands—you want both thick and thin pieces of pork. Add the barbecue sauce and toss with the meat.

9 **SANDWICHES** Top each slider bun with some pork, followed by the slaw.

NOTE *You can make the barbecue sauce up to a week in advance. Cover and refrigerate until ready to use, then reheat before serving. You can make the slaw a day in advance; just don't add the dressing until you are ready to serve it.*

ROGAN GHOSH

GF (LAMB STEW)

This is one of the best-known dishes from Kashmir, the northern state in India that borders Pakistan (and is claimed by both countries). It's a Persian-influenced dish that is rich in spices, so be sure to toast the spices in order to maximize flavor.

½ cup (125 mL) **Plain Yogurt** (page 40) or store-bought

1 2-inch (5 cm) piece **ginger**, peeled and minced

10 **garlic cloves**, minced

1 tablespoon (15 mL) **kosher salt** (approx.)

1 teaspoon (5 mL) ground **turmeric**

1 teaspoon (5 mL) crushed **black peppercorns**

2 pounds (1 kg) trimmed boneless **lamb shoulder**, cut into 2-inch (5 cm) pieces

4 **green cardamom pods**, crushed

1 2-inch (5 cm) **cinnamon stick**

1 tablespoon (15 mL) **coriander seeds**

2 teaspoons (10 mL) **cumin seeds**

2 teaspoons (10 mL) **smoked paprika**

½ teaspoon (2 mL) ground **cloves**

2 tablespoons (30 mL) **vegetable oil**

2 large **onions**, chopped

2 **red** or **yellow bell pepper**s, finely chopped

2 **serrano chiles**, minced

1 can (28 oz/796 mL) whole **tomatoes** (with juice), roughly chopped

1 Whisk together the yogurt, ginger, garlic, salt, turmeric and peppercorns in a large bowl. Add the lamb and, using your hands, rub the marinade all over the meat until it is evenly coated. Cover and refrigerate for a minimum of 8 hours or up to 16 hours.

2 Using the Sauté function on High, heat the cardamom pods, cinnamon stick, coriander seeds, cumin seeds, paprika and cloves; cook, stirring frequently, for about 1 minute, until fragrant. Transfer to a small bowl.

3 Using the Sauté function on High, heat the oil in the inner pot for about 1 minute, until shimmering. Add the onions; cook, stirring occasionally, for 4 minutes, just until softened. Add the bell peppers and chiles; cook for about 2 minutes, stirring occasionally, just until softened. Add the toasted spice mixture.

4 Add the tomatoes (with juice), and the lamb and its marinade; stir to combiner. Secure the lid and cook on high pressure for 20 minutes.

5 Let the pressure release naturally for 10 minutes, then quick-release the remaining pressure.

6 Remove the lid and stir. Using the Sauté function on Low, simmer for 3 minutes, stirring occasionally, until the liquid has reduced and the sauce has thickened. Taste and add additional salt, if needed.

Bafat
PORK RIBS

(SPICY RIBS)

These ribs come together in minutes, rather than hours on the grill, and boast the floral heat of a bafat spice blend, which comes from Mangalore, on the southwestern coast of India. Mangaloreans are famous for their bafat-seasoned pork curry, and the spices also happen to be pretty fantastic on a slab of pork ribs. If you are nervous about the dish being too spicy for you, use the bafat spice powder on the ribs but not in the sauce.

Coffee/spice grinder

Instant Pot trivet

½ cup (125 mL) **Bafat Spice Powder** (see page 28), divided

1 tablespoon (15 mL) **smoked paprika**

1 tablespoon (15 mL) **kosher salt**

2 racks **pork baby back ribs** (about 2 pounds/1 kg each)

½ cup (125 mL) **apple cider vinegar**

½ cup (125 mL) **water**

1 cup (250 mL) **orange juice**

½ cup (125 mL) **tamarind paste**

½ cup (125 mL) **ketchup**

¼ cup (60 mL) **honey**

2 tablespoons (30 mL) **soy sauce**

1 Combine 6 tablespoons (90 mL) of the bafat spice powder, paprika and salt in a small bowl.

2 Place the ribs on a clean work surface. Rub the spice mixture all over the meat.

3 Place the trivet in the inner pot. Pour in the vinegar and water.

4 Place the ribs on the trivet, positioning the curve of each rack against the wall of the inner pot. Secure the lid and cook on high pressure for 28 minutes.

5 Meanwhile, preheat the oven to 450°F (230°C).

6 Once the ribs are cooked, let the pressure release naturally for 10 minutes, then quick-release the remaining pressure.

7 Meanwhile, in a small saucepan over low heat, whisk together the remaining 2 tablespoons (30 mL) bafat spice powder and the orange juice, tamarind paste, ketchup, honey and soy sauce. Simmer for about 15 minutes, until reduced and thick. Set aside.

8 Remove the ribs from the inner pot and brush both sides with the sauce. (Discard the liquid from the pot.) Place the ribs on a rimmed baking sheet with the meaty side up. Bake in the preheated oven for 5 minutes, until the sauce begins to brown. Remove from the oven and serve with the remaining sauce alongside.

TEA-BRAISED
LAMB
STEW

GF

Here's a stew full of spice but not heat. The fruity notes from the tea and the orange make a perfect contrast for the lamb. If you have some Clementine Ginger Chutney (page 85) on hand, use 1/2 cup (125 mL) of that instead of the minced orange, for even more flavor. Don't skip seasoning the lamb in advance; it really helps meld the meat with the flavors of the stew.

1	tablespoon (15 mL) **kosher salt**
1	teaspoon (5 mL) **smoked paprika**
3	teaspoons (15 mL) **Garam Masala** (page 24) or store-bought, divided
1	teaspoon (5 mL) freshly ground **black pepper**
3	pounds (1.5 kg) trimmed boneless **lamb stewing meat**, cut into 1-inch (2.5 cm) pieces
3	tablespoons (45 mL) **vegetable oil**, divided
2	**onions**, thinly sliced
2	teaspoons (10 mL) ground **cinnamon**
1	teaspoon (5 mL) **Kashmiri chili powder**
½	teaspoon (2 mL) ground **cloves**
6	**garlic cloves**, minced
1½	cups (375 mL) strong brewed **Assam**, **Darjeeling** or **black tea**
½	**orange**, peel and flesh, minced
1	can (14 oz/398 mL) diced **tomatoes** (with juice)

1 Combine the salt, paprika, 1 teaspoon (5 mL) garam masala and pepper in a large bowl; add the lamb and toss to coat evenly. Cover and refrigerate for 1 hour or up to 8 hours.

2 Using the Sauté function on High, heat 1 tablespoon (15 mL) oil in the inner pot for about 1 minute, until shimmering. Working in 3 batches, add the lamb and cook for about 5 to 6 minutes, until browned on all sides, adding the remaining oil as needed. Transfer the browned lamb to a bowl.

3 Add the onions to the inner pot and cook, stirring occasionally, for about 4 minutes, until softened. Stir in the remaining 2 teaspoons (10 mL) garam masala, cinnamon, chili powder, cloves and garlic; cook for about 1 minute, until fragrant. Add the tea; using a wooden spoon, stir, scraping up any browned bits on the bottom of the pot. Add the minced orange and tomatoes (with juice); stir until combined.

4 Secure the lid and cook on high pressure for 23 minutes.

5 Once the cooking is complete, let the pressure release naturally for 10 minutes, then quick-release the remaining pressure.

6 Remove the lid and stir. Using the Sauté function on Normal, simmer for about 5 minutes, stirring occasionally, until thickened slightly.

COCONUT CILANTRO STEAMED FISH GF

Mumbai is home to a large Parsi community—people descended from followers of the prophet Zoroaster who settled in India after fleeing persecution in Persia about a thousand years ago. If you go to a Parsi wedding, chances are you'll be served this dish of mild white fish seasoned with coconut cilantro chutney, then wrapped in banana leaves and grilled or steamed. Banana leaves definitely up the ante on the presentation, but if you can't find them, simply wrap each fillet in parchment paper, then foil. I like to serve this fish over coconut rice for an extra coconutty meal, but any rice will do.

Instant Pot trivet

- 4 skinless **fish fillets** (whitefish, halibut or cod), each about 6 oz (175 g)
- 2 teaspoons (10 mL) ground **turmeric**
- 1 teaspoon (5 mL) **kosher salt**
- 4 **banana leaves** or 12-inch (30 cm) squares parchment paper
- 2 cups (500 mL) **Coconut Cilantro Chutney** (page 92) or store-bought
- 1 cup (250 mL) **water**

1 Place the fish on a plate and season on both sides with the turmeric and salt.

2 Place the banana leaves on a clean work surface. Remove the center rib of each leaf. Spread about 2 tablespoons (30 mL) chutney in the center of each piece, then place a fish fillet on top. Spread about 2 tablespoons (30 mL) chutney all over the top of each fillet, covering completely. Fold the top piece of the leaf over the fish, then fold in the sides and bottom, wrapping it up into a parcel. (If you are using parchment paper, add a layer of foil over it to enclose the entire parcel.)

3 Pour the water into the inner pot and place the trivet inside. Place the fish parcels on the trivet. Secure the lid and, using the Steam function, steam the fish for 10 minutes.

4 Once the cooking is complete, quick-release the steam.

5 Remove the packets and serve.

ORANGE CUMIN
SALMON.

GF

I learned that cumin is an ideal seasoning for fish while eating grouper with an orange cumin sauce at Hartwood, a wonderful restaurant in Tulum, Mexico. I decided to Indian-ify it and use salmon instead of grouper, because its firmer texture holds up a bit better under pressure cooking. The coriander lends a floral note that really works with the sweet-tart orange sauce.

1	tablespoon (15 mL) ground **cumin**
1	tablespoon (15 mL) ground **coriander**
2	teaspoons (10 mL) **Garam Masala** (page 24) or store-bought
1	teaspoon (5 mL) **kosher salt** (approx.)
4	**salmon fillets** (each about 6 oz/175 g and 1 inch/2.5 cm thick), skin removed
1	tablespoon (15 mL) **ghee**
¼	cup (60 mL) **orange juice**
3	tablespoons (45 mL) **jaggery** or **brown sugar**
2	teaspoons (10 mL) freshly ground **black pepper**
2	teaspoons (10 mL) freshly squeezed **lime juice**
¼	cup (60 mL) fresh **cilantro** leaves
	Kosher salt

1 Combine the cumin, coriander, garam masala and salt in a small bowl. Sprinkle over both sides of the salmon.

2 Using the Sauté function on High, heat the ghee in the inner pot for about 1 minute, until shimmering. Place the salmon in the inner pot. Pour the orange juice around the fish, secure the lid, and cook on low pressure for 1 minute (you can also cook on high pressure for 0 minutes if you are using thick salmon fillets that won't overcook as easily).

3 Once the cooking is complete, let the pressure release naturally for 4 minutes, then quick-release the remaining pressure.

4 Remove the lid. Using a spatula, transfer the salmon to a serving platter. Add the jaggery to the inner pot and, using the Sauté function on High, cook for about 1 minute, until the sugar is melted. Add the pepper and lime juice; cook, stirring constantly, for about 2 minutes, until the jaggery begins to caramelize and thicken. Simmer for about 2 to 3 minutes to reduce the sauce until somewhat thickened. Season to taste with salt.

5 Pour the sauce over the salmon and garnish with cilantro; serve.

SRI LANKAN CRAB CURRY.

GF

If India seems fascinating and exotic to you, well, that's what Sri Lanka is to me. I've never been there, even though it's not far off the Indian coast and I've always wanted to go. So I was really excited to meet Sam Fore, the chef/owner of Tuk Tuk, a Sri Lankan restaurant in my hometown in Kentucky. I wish that Sam and her restaurant had been around while I was growing up, but she's made up for that by sharing with me her mother's crab curry recipe, which I've adapted for the Instant Pot.

4 pounds (2 kg) whole live **blue crabs** or **king crab legs** (see Note, right)

3 tablespoons (45 mL) **Sri Lankan Curry Powder** (page 27)

3 tablespoons (45 mL) **ghee** or **vegetable oil**

1 **onion**, finely chopped

12 fresh **curry leaves**, torn into pieces

1 tablespoon (15 mL) **kosher salt**

1 tablespoon (15 mL) **brown mustard seeds**

2 **serrano chiles**, minced

4 **garlic cloves**, minced

1 tablespoon (15 mL) minced **ginger**

¼ cup (60 mL) unsweetened **coconut flakes**, toasted (page 29)

2 tablespoons (30 mL) **tamarind paste**

1 can (14 oz/398 mL) full-fat **coconut milk**

2 cups (500 mL) **water**

2 tablespoons (30 mL) freshly squeezed **lime juice**

1   Place the live crabs in a large bowl filled with ice water for 30 minutes (this puts them into a stupor). Hold each crab by the bottom, shell side up, then tear off the upper shell. Rinse the crabs under cold running water while you remove the gills and the guts (everything but the meat), then cut each crab in half. (If you are using king crab legs, use a knife or scissors to cut down one side of each leg to expose the meat).

2   Place the curry powder in a large bowl. Add the crabs and toss to coat.

3   Using the Sauté function on High, heat the ghee in the inner pot for about 1 minute, until shimmering. Add the onion and cook for about 4 minutes, stirring occasionally, until softened. Stir in the curry leaves, salt, mustard seeds, chiles, garlic, ginger and coconut; cook for about 1 minute, until fragrant. Stir in the tamarind paste, coconut milk and water.

4   Add the crabs, stirring to coat in the sauce. Secure the lid and cook on low pressure for 8 minutes.

5   Once the crabs are cooked, quick-release the pressure.

6   Remove the lid. Using the Sauté function on Normal, simmer for about 2 minutes, until the sauce has thickened. Add the lime juice and serve, with plenty of napkins.

NOTE *You can use split crab legs or jumbo shrimp (U/10) in this recipe. Just reduce the pressure-cooking time to 5 minutes.*

GOAN SHRIMP GF CURRY

Goa is famous for its coconuts, seafood and spices. All three come together in this curry, which is beachy and delicious enough to be something you might imagine eating happily on a desert island, should you find yourself stranded on one (with an Instant Pot, of course).

2 tablespoons (30 mL) **ghee** or **coconut oil**

6 fresh **curry leaves**, torn into pieces

1 cup (250 mL) unsweetened **coconut flakes**

1 teaspoon (5 mL) ground **cumin**

3 **dried red chiles**, torn into pieces

3 plum **tomatoes**, chopped

2 **onions**, sliced

1 tablespoon (15 mL) ground **coriander**

2 teaspoons (10 mL) **kosher salt**

1 teaspoon (5 mL) ground **turmeric**

1 teaspoon (5 mL) **Kashmiri chili powder**

½ teaspoon (2 mL) ground **fenugreek**

1 **serrano chile**, minced

1 tablespoon (15 mL) minced **ginger**

3 **garlic cloves**, minced

1 can (14 oz/398 mL) full-fat **coconut milk**

1 pound (500 g) raw **shrimp** (size 16/20 or larger) thawed if frozen, peeled and deveined

2 teaspoons (10 mL) freshly squeezed **lemon juice**

1 Using the Sauté function on High, heat the ghee in the inner pot for 1 minute, until shimmering. Add the curry leaves; cook for about 1 minute, until sizzling.

2 Add the coconut, cumin, dried chiles, tomatoes, onions, coriander, salt, turmeric, chili powder and fenugreek; cook, stirring frequently, for about 2 minutes, until the onions begin to soften. Stir in the serrano chile, ginger and garlic; cook for about 1 minute, until fragrant. Add the coconut milk; using a wooden spoon, stir, scraping up any browned bits on the bottom of the pot.

3 Stir in the shrimp. Secure the lid and cook on low pressure for 5 minutes (you can also cook on high pressure for 3 minutes).

4 Once the cooking is complete, quick-release the pressure.

5 Remove the lid and stir in the lemon juice. If the sauce is too thin for your liking, remove the shrimp from the pot. Using the Sauté function on High, simmer the curry for 5 minutes to reduce the sauce to the desired consistency. Return the shrimp to the pot before serving.

Breads

PANCAKES

and

CREPES

MAKING IDLIS, DOSAS & UTTAPAMS

IDLIS (steamed fermented lentil cakes), dosas (savory crepes) and uttapams (savory pancakes) are standard breakfasts and lunches in South Indian homes. They are all made from the same batter, which can take days to ferment, especially if the weather where you live isn't very tropical or India-ish. But the Instant Pot makes it easier, creating the warm, humid environment you need for fermentation in as little as nine hours.

Once you make the batter, the rest is easy. But there are a few rules:

1 Rinse the rice and dal thoroughly before soaking.

2 Soak the rice and dal in distilled water, not tap water
   (the chlorine in tap water inhibits fermentation).

3 Use ice-cold water when grinding the rice and dal.

4 Ferment the batter in a warm place (hint: your Instant Pot!).

5 Make sure the batter is at room temperature before cooking with it.

6 If you want to make idlis, use the batter within two days of making it;
   it will be light and fluffy.

7 Thin the batter with a little water to make dosas, uttapams or appams.

8 If your idlis are tough, then make dosas and uttapams
   (tell everyone that was your intention from the beginning).

PREP	YOGURT	TOTAL	MAKES
15 MIN	**9 HR**	**35 MIN** (PLUS 17 HR INACTIVE TIME)	**9 CUPS** (2.25 L)

VEG **GF** **V** IDLI, DOSA AND UTTAPAM

BATTER

This batter can be used for idlis, dosas or uttapams and is pretty straightforward, but particular. Make sure you buy urad dal without the skins. Don't even think about using tap water instead of distilled, skipping the fenugreek or using iodized salt. And the batter won't ferment enough if you don't carefully follow the recipe or the rules on page 234.

High-powered blender

- 1 cup (250 mL) whole **urad dal** (without the skins), rinsed
- 1 teaspoon (5 mL) **fenugreek seeds**
  Distilled or bottled **water** (see Notes)
- 4 cups (1 L) **Idli rice**, rinsed (see Notes)
  Ice cubes
- 1 cup (250 mL) iced distilled **water** (approx.)
- 1 teaspoon (5 mL) **baking soda**
- 1 teaspoon (5 mL) **kosher salt**

1 Combine the urad dal and fenugreek seeds in a large bowl. Add enough distilled water to cover by 2 inches (5 cm). Soak for at least 8 hours or up to 12 hours.

2 Place the rice in a separate bowl and add enough distilled water to cover by 2 inches (5 cm). Soak for at least 8 hours and up to 12 hours.

3 Strain the dal mixture, reserving the soaking water. Add ice to the soaking water to cool it down. Transfer the dal mixture to a high-powered blender (or a wet-dry grinder, if you happen to be old-school). Add ½ cup (125 mL) of the soaking water. Start blending the dal on low speed, then move up to high speed as it breaks down; you'll need to blend it for about 5 to 10 minutes (depending on the power of your blender). Add more soaking water as needed to help blend the dal into a smooth, runny batter and to prevent the blender motor from burning out. You should have 2 cups (500 mL) dal batter; add more soaking water if needed to achieve that volume. Transfer the batter to the inner pot.

Recipe continues . . .

4 Strain the rice, discard the soaking water, and transfer the soaked rice to the blender. Add iced distilled water. Start blending the rice on low speed, then move up to high speed as it breaks down; you'll need to blend it for about 5 minutes (depending on the power of your blender). Add more ice water as needed to create a thin, runny batter. You should have 5 cups (1.25 L) rice batter; whisk in more ice water if needed to achieve that volume.

5 Add the rice batter to the dal batter in the inner pot. Add the baking soda and salt; stir the batters together until fully combined.

6 Remove the sealing ring from the lid. Secure the lid and, using the Yogurt function on Low, ferment the batter for 9 hours.

7 Turn off the Instant Pot and remove the lid. The batter should have risen to the 10-cup (2.5 L) mark. If not, use the Yogurt function to ferment the batter for another 2 to 3 hours, making sure not to let the batter rise too high—it could essentially glue the lid onto the pot (I'm serious).

8 Use the batter immediately (or within 2 days if you want to make idlis), or transfer to an airtight container and refrigerate for up to 1 week. For best results, bring the batter back to room temperature before using it.

NOTES

Distilled water is purified water stripped of contaminants and minerals. Not all bottled waters are distilled, so check the label.

Idli rice is parboiled white rice that works especially well for making idli and dosa batter. It is available in Indian grocery stores.

IDLIS

VEG **GF** **V** (STEAMED FERMENTED LENTIL CAKES)

If you want to make idlis, use the batter on page 233 within two days of fermentation. That will give you lighter and fluffier idlis instead of leaden lumps that make aunties give you the side-eye as they pity you (oh, I've been there). I serve these with Cherry Tomato Chutney (page 86), Coconut Cilantro Chutney (page 92) or, in winter, Winter Squash Sambar (page 238). Once you get the hang of making idlis, feel free to play with the seasonings—you can add 1 tablespoon (15 mL) turmeric, chopped onion or cilantro and minced chiles to the batter before steaming it.

6-inch (15 cm) idli maker, greased (see Note)

4   cups (1 L) **Idli, Dosa and Uttapam Batter** (page 235)
1   cup (250 mL) boiling **water**

1   Spoon enough batter into each idli mold to reach the top.

2   Pour the boiling water into the inner pot; then add the filled idli maker. Secure the lid and set the pressure valve to Venting. Using the Steam function, steam for 10 minutes. (The Instant Pot timer will not work while venting, so you'll need to set a separate timer.)

3   Once the cooking is complete, quick-release the pressure.

4   Remove the idli maker from the inner pot. Pop the idlis out of the molds and serve.

NOTE *You can buy idli makers from Indian groceries or online. Look for one that is 6 inches (15 cm) in diameter, so it will fit inside the inner pot.*

IDLIS WITH WINTER SQUASH

VEG GF V

SAMBAR

Idlis are somewhat plain, which makes them the perfect foil for sambar, a brothy, spicy sauce. You can eat it as a soup, even without the idlis.

Coffee/spice grinder

- 2 **dried red chiles**
- 1 teaspoon (5 mL) **coriander seeds**
- 1 teaspoon (5 mL) **cumin seeds**
- ½ teaspoon (2 mL) **fenugreek seeds**
- ½ teaspoon (2 mL) **black peppercorns**
- ½ teaspoon (2 mL) ground **turmeric**
- 1 tablespoon (15 mL) **vegetable oil**
- 1 **onion**, chopped
- 1 cup (250 mL) **toor dal**, rinsed
- 1 teaspoon (5 mL) **mustard seeds**
- 12 fresh **curry leaves**, torn into pieces
- Pinch **asafoetida**
- 1 **serrano chile**, minced
- 1 tablespoon (15 mL) minced **ginger**
- 1 cup (250 mL) **water**
- 2 **tomatoes**, chopped
- 2 teaspoons (10 mL) **kosher salt**
- 1 tablespoon (15 mL) **tamarind concentrate**
- 6 ounces (175 g) peeled **pumpkin** or **butternut squash**, chopped
- 12 cooked **Idlis** (page 237) or store-bought, warmed

1   Combine the dried chiles, coriander seeds, cumin seeds, fenugreek seeds, peppercorns and turmeric in a coffee/spice grinder. Grind to a powder.

2   Transfer the spices to a dry skillet and cook over medium heat, shaking the pan frequently to distribute them, for about 2 minutes, until toasted. Remove from the heat.

3   Using the Sauté function on High, heat the oil in the inner pot for about 1 minute, until shimmering. Add the onion; cook, stirring frequently, for about 4 minutes, until softened.

4   Stir in the toor dal, toasted spice mixture, mustard seeds, curry leaves, asafoetida, serrano chile and ginger. Cook, stirring, for about 1 minute, until fragrant. Stir in the water, using a wooden spoon to scrape up any browned bits from the bottom of the inner pot. Stir in the tomatoes, salt, tamarind concentrate and pumpkin. Secure the lid and cook on high pressure for 8 minutes.

5   Once the cooking is complete, quick-release the pressure.

6   Remove the lid and stir the sambar. Spoon into a bowl and serve alongside the idlis.

TOTAL
35 MIN
(PLUS ABOUT
18 HRS FOR THE
BATTER)

MAKES
8 DOSAS

DOSAS

VEG GF V **(FERMENTED LENTIL AND RICE CREPES)**

Dosas are one of the stars of South Indian cuisine, especially at restaurants that specialize in making the giant, table-sized paper versions (if you haven't seen one, I suggest you Google it right now). You should start with making normal plate-sized dosas, and keep practicing until you get the technique down. You can fill your dosas with just about anything: leftover grilled, stewed or roasted vegetables, cheese or whatever else is calling to you from your fridge (yes, spaghetti sauce dosas can be done).

½ cup (125 mL) **vegetable oil** or **coconut oil**, divided (approx.)

2 cups (500 mL) **Idli, Dosa and Uttapam Batter** (page 235)

1 Heat a large cast-iron or heavy-bottomed nonstick skillet over medium heat. Brush the skillet lightly with 1 teaspoon (5 mL) oil.

2 Ladle about ¼ cup (60 mL) batter into the center of the skillet. Using the bottom of the ladle, spread the batter around the pan into a crepe about 8 inches (20 cm) wide, tilting the pan to even it out (you want a very thin layer). Cook for about 3 to 4 minutes, until browned and crispy on the bottom.

3 Spoon 1 teaspoon (5 mL) oil over the dosa, gently spreading it around. Use a thin spatula to loosen the dosa around the edges and carefully remove it from the pan; transfer to a plate. Repeat with the remaining batter and oil, placing each dosa on a separate plate once it is cooked. Top with your choice of filling (see pages 243 to 246 for options), fold it in half, and serve.

PREP
10 MIN

TOTAL
40 MIN
(PLUS ABOUT
19 HR FOR THE
DOSAS AND
INACTIVE TIME)

MAKES
8 DOSAS

RAVA DOSAS

VEG **GF** (ONION DOSAS)

We ate these dosas so often when I was a kid that I thought they were named for Ravi, my oldest brother. It's kind of embarrassing to think that I was probably about 20 years old when I realized the name was *rava*, not Ravi. I still often include them on a menu for sentimental reasons—and because I love the simplicity of a dosa with just chiles and onions; you can really taste the glorious tang of the dosa batter.

2 cups (500 mL) **Idli, Dosa and Uttapam Batter** (page 235)

1 small **red onion**, minced

1 **serrano chile**, minced

1 teaspoon (5 mL) minced **ginger**

1 teaspoon (5 mL) **cumin seeds**

8 fresh **curry leaves**, torn into pieces

Water

½ cup (125 mL) **vegetable oil**, divided (approx.)

½ cup (125 mL) **Coconut Cilantro Chutney** (page 92) or store-bought

1 Whisk together the batter, onion, chile, ginger, cumin seeds and curry leaves in a large bowl. Add ¼ cup (60 mL) water, or more as needed, to create a thin but not watery batter. Let stand for 30 minutes.

2 Meanwhile, heat a large cast-iron or heavy-bottomed skillet over medium heat. Brush the pan with 1 teaspoon (5 mL) oil. Whisk the batter, then ladle ¼ cup (60 mL) into the pan, making sure to include some of the onion and chile. Using the bottom of the ladle, spread the batter around into a crepe about 8 inches (20 cm) wide. Cook for about 3 to 4 minutes, until the dosa is browned and crispy on the bottom.

3 Spoon 1 teaspoon (5 mL) oil over the dosa, gently spreading it around. Use a thin spatula to loosen the dosa around the edges and carefully remove it from the pan; transfer to a plate and fold in half. Repeat with the remaining batter and oil. Serve 2 dosas per person, with chutney on the side for dipping.

PREP	SAUTÉ	MANUAL	RELEASE	TOTAL	MAKES
10 MIN	**6 MIN**	**1 MIN**	**QUICK**	**20 MIN** (PLUS ABOUT 18½ HR FOR THE DOSAS)	**8 DOSAS**

Asparagus VEG GF V MUSHROOM DOSAS

When spring hits, I want to eat as much asparagus as possible—it's such a relief after five months of root vegetables. I used to make asparagus crepes when I was a cook at a hotel in Maine, so it was natural to create an Indian version of that dish by filling dosas with asparagus and mushrooms. The coriander and lemon make this especially nice for Sunday brunch.

2 tablespoons (30 mL) **vegetable oil**

1 **onion**, thinly sliced

2 cups (500 mL) sliced **mushrooms**

2 teaspoons (10 mL) **kosher salt**

2 teaspoons (10 mL) ground **coriander**

1 teaspoon (5 mL) ground **cumin**

½ cup (125 mL) boiling **water**

2 pounds (1 kg) **asparagus**, trimmed

2 tablespoons (30 mL) grated **lemon zest**

8 cooked **Dosas** (page 240), warmed

1   Using the Sauté function on High, heat the oil in the inner pot for about 1 minute, until shimmering. Add the onion, mushrooms and salt; cook, stirring, for about 4 minutes, until softened. Stir in the coriander and cumin; cook, stirring, for about 1 minute, until fragrant.

2   Stir in the boiling water, using a wooden spoon to scrape up any browned bits from the bottom of the pot. Add the asparagus, cutting up the spears so they fit in the inner pot.

3   Secure the lid and cook on low pressure for 1 minute (you can also cook on high pressure for 0 minutes).

4   Once the cooking is complete, quick-release the pressure.

5   Transfer the vegetables to a large bowl. Stir in the lemon zest, then divide the mixture among the 8 dosas. Fold each dosa over the vegetables and serve.

Zucchini,

VEG · GF · V **EGGPLANT AND CORN**

DOSAS

This is a nice summery dosa, which is perfect for when you have loads of zucchini, corn and eggplant and want to show them off. (I like to add plenty of vegetables to balance out my dosa habit.)

2 tablespoons (30 mL) **vegetable oil**

1 **onion**, chopped

1 tablespoon (15 mL) **kosher salt**

1 **serrano chile**, minced

8 fresh **curry leaves**, torn into pieces

1 tablespoon (15 mL) **Curry Powder** (page 23) or store-bought

1 cup (250 mL) fresh or frozen **corn** kernels, thawed if frozen

2 **zucchini**, chopped

1 small (8 oz/250 g) **eggplant**, chopped

½ cup (125 mL) **water**

½ cup (125 mL) chopped fresh **basil**

8 cooked **Dosas** (page 240), warmed

1 Using the Sauté function on High, heat the oil in the inner pot for about 1 minute, until shimmering. Add the onion and salt; cook, stirring, for about 4 minutes, until the onion is softened. Stir in the chile, curry leaves, curry powder, corn, zucchini and eggplant; cook, stirring, for about 1 minute, until fragrant.

2 Add the water and stir, using a wooden spoon to scrape up any browned bits from the bottom of the pot.

3 Secure the lid and cook on low pressure for 3 minutes (you can also cook on high pressure for 0 minutes).

4 Once the cooking is complete, quick-release the pressure.

5 Stir in the basil, then divide the vegetable mixture among the 8 dosas. Fold each dosa over the vegetables and serve.

MASALA DOSAS

(POTATO DOSAS)

I'm not sure there's anything as mouth-watering as the smell of spiced potatoes and onions frying in ghee. I regularly woke up to that on Sunday mornings when I was a kid, and it often meant we were having masala dosas—perhaps the most classic dosas—for lunch. These days I'm more likely to eat this for Sunday dinner instead. The crisp dosa and spicy potatoes pair pretty perfectly with a movie and a glass of wine, and it's just as comforting as the long, lazy Sunday lunches with my family.

1½	pounds (750 g) **yellow-fleshed potatoes**, quartered
1	cup (250 mL) **water**
3	tablespoons (45 mL) **vegetable oil**
2	teaspoons (10 mL) **mustard seeds**
2	teaspoons (10 mL) **cumin seeds**
2	**onions**, chopped
2	**green Thai chiles**, minced
2	teaspoons (10 mL) **kosher salt** (approx.)
1	teaspoon (5 mL) ground **turmeric**
	Pinch **asafoetida**
8	fresh **curry leaves**, torn into pieces
1	tablespoon (15 mL) minced **ginger**
4	**garlic cloves**, minced
½	cup (125 mL) chopped fresh **cilantro**
8	cooked **Dosas** (page 240), warmed

1 Place the potatoes and water in the inner pot. Secure the lid and cook on low pressure for 12 minutes (you can also cook on high pressure for 8 minutes).

2 Once the cooking is complete, quick-release the pressure. Using a slotted spoon, transfer the potatoes to a large bowl, reserving about ¼ cup (60 mL) of the cooking water.

3 Using the Sauté function on High, heat the oil in the inner pot for about 1 minute, until shimmering. Add the mustard seeds and cumin seeds; cook, stirring, for about 1 minute, until the mustard seeds begin to pop. Add the onions, chiles and salt; cook, stirring occasionally, for about 4 minutes, until the onions have softened. Stir in the turmeric, asafoetida, curry leaves, ginger and garlic; cook, stirring, for 1 minute, until fragrant and the curry leaves are sizzling.

4 Return the potatoes to the inner pot and mash them slightly with the back of a wooden spoon, adding some of the reserved cooking water if they seem dry. Stir the mashed potatoes in with the onions and spices. Season with additional salt, if needed, and stir in the cilantro.

5 Spoon even portions of the potato mixture into the middle of each dosa. Fold the dosa over the filling and serve.

APPAMS

   (FERMENTED RICE AND COCONUT PANCAKES)

Appams are crepes similar to dosas and uttapams, but with the addition of coconut milk (everything in Kerala is coconutty—it's a rule). Once you get the hang of making these, they'll become a regular craving, so feel free to double this recipe if you like. Eat them with chutney; I like Coconut Cilantro Chutney (page 92) or Spicy South Indian Lime Pickle (page 82).

1⅔ cups (400 mL) **Idli, Dosa and Uttapam Batter** (page 235)

⅓ cup (75 mL) full-fat **coconut milk**

1 teaspoon (5 mL) powdered **jaggery** or **brown sugar**

1 tablespoon (15 mL) unsweetened **coconut flakes**
 Water (optional)

1 Whisk together the batter, coconut milk, jaggery and coconut in a large bowl until smooth. The batter should be thin but not watery; add a small amount of water if it is too thick.

2 Heat a small (6-inch/15 cm) nonstick skillet over medium heat. Ladle about ⅓ cup (75 mL) batter into the center of the skillet. Tilt the pan to spread the batter up the sides. The batter should be very thin around the edges and have a very shallow bowl shape toward the center.

3 Cover the skillet and cook for about 2 to 3 minutes, until the edges of the appam are browned and the center is set. Use a thin spatula to carefully peel the appam from the skillet without destroying the lacy edges; transfer to a plate. Repeat with the remaining batter, placing each cooked appam on a separate plate.

4 Serve the appams with any curry or chutney.

PREP
10 MIN

TOTAL
20 MIN
(PLUS ABOUT
18 HR FOR
THE BATTER)

SERVES
4

CARROT BEET CILANTRO
UTTAPAMS

 (SAVORY VEGETABLE PANCAKES)

I joke that I change my idli plans to make uttapams when I can't get my batter to work out, but the truth is I think these savory pancakes are one of the best South Indian treats. You'll find them in restaurants as large as a dinner plate, but I like to make them the size of blinis and serve them as cocktail party snacks. It turns out that uttapams are actually pretty fancy when they're gussied up and served with a glass of Champagne.

3 tablespoons (45 mL) **vegetable oil**, divided

1 cup (250 mL) **Idli, Dosa and Uttapam Batter** (page 235)

1 small **red onion**, minced

1 small **red beet**, grated

2 **carrots**, grated

1 **serrano chile**, minced

½ cup (125 mL) **Coconut Cilantro Chutney** (page 92) or store-bought

1 Heat 1 tablespoon (15 mL) oil in a large cast-iron or heavy-bottomed nonstick skillet over medium heat for 1 minute, tilting the skillet to spread it around, until shimmering. Working in batches, drop 1 tablespoon (15 mL) batter into the skillet for each uttapam, spacing 1 inch (2.5 cm) apart; you should be able to cook 4 at a time.

2 Working quickly, sprinkle a little onion, beet, carrot and chile on top of each pancake before the top cooks. Cook for 1 to 2 minutes, until brown and crisp on the bottom; then flip and cook for 1 minute more, until browned on the other side.

3 Transfer the cooked uttapams to a platter. Repeat with the remaining batter and vegetables, adding more oil to the pan as needed. Serve topped with a dollop of chutney.

DHOKLA

  (CHICKPEA FLOUR CAKE)

Dhokla is a mild cake made with besan, or chickpea flour. It's usually cut into small pieces and served plain, but since it reminds me a bit of polenta, I give it a topping of rapini sautéed with spices and cooked in coconut milk to make it more substantial.

Instant Pot trivet

7-inch (18 cm) metal cake pan, greased

1½ cups (375 mL) **besan** (chickpea flour)

3 tablespoons (45 mL) **Plain Yogurt** (page 40) or store-bought

4 teaspoons (20 mL) **kosher salt**, divided

1 teaspoon (5 mL) granulated **sugar**

1 cup (250 mL) hot **water**

2 teaspoons (10 mL) minced **ginger**

5 tablespoons (75 mL) **vegetable oil**, divided

1 cup (250 mL) **water**

1 teaspoon (5 mL) **baking soda**

½ teaspoon (2 mL) **citric acid** powder

3 tablespoons (45 mL) **vegetable oil**

1 tablespoon (15 mL) **brown mustard seeds**

1 tablespoon (15 mL) **cumin seeds**

1 **serrano chile**, minced

4 **garlic cloves**, minced

2 cups (500 mL) chopped **rapini**

1 cup (250 mL) full-fat **coconut milk**

2 tablespoons (30 mL) unsweetened **coconut flakes**

1 Combine the besan, yogurt, 2 teaspoons (10 mL) salt and sugar in an insert pan or a clean metal, ceramic or glass bowl small enough to fit in the inner pot. Whisk in 1 cup (250 mL) hot water.

2 Place the trivet in the inner pot and place the bowl of batter on the trivet. Secure the lid. Select the Yogurt function on Normal and set the time to 4 hours.

3 Remove the batter from the inner pot and whisk in the ginger and 2 tablespoons (30 mL) of the oil. Empty the inner pot.

4 Using the Sauté function on High, heat 1 cup (250 mL) water in the inner pot for about 4 minutes, until boiling. Meanwhile, whisk the baking soda and citric acid into the batter (it will bubble up for a few seconds).

5 Pour the batter into the prepared baking pan, smoothing the top. Place the pan on the trivet in the inner pot and secure the lid. Using the Steam function, steam for 20 minutes, keeping the pressure valve in the Venting position (the Instant Pot timer will not work while venting, so you'll need to set a separate timer).

6 Once the cooking is complete, quick-release the pressure. Check the dhokla; it should be puffy and dry on top and a knife inserted in the center should come out clean. If it is undercooked, steam for another 5 minutes. Remove the pan and let cool to room temperature. Empty the inner pot and wipe it clean.

7 Using the Sauté function on High, heat the remaining 3 tablespoons (45 mL) oil in the inner pot for about 1 minute, until shimmering. Add the mustard seeds, cumin seeds and remaining 2 teaspoons (10 mL) salt; cook, stirring, for about 1 minute, until the mustard seeds begin to pop. Stir in the chile, garlic and rapini; cook, stirring, for 2 minutes. Add the coconut milk; simmer, stirring frequently, for 3 minutes.

8 Slice the dhokla into 6 squares or wedges and place on a plate. Spoon the rapini mixture over the dhokla, garnish with the coconut flakes, and serve.

PREP
10 MIN

YOGURT
1 HR

TOTAL
1 HR 30 MIN

MAKES
8 NAAN

NAAN.

VEG

One of the most important parts of bread baking is the proofing process, which you can do in an Instant Pot using the Yogurt function. The dough rises in less time than usual, making a flatbread like naan something you can pull off even on a weeknight. Searing the naan with ghee in a super-hot pan isn't traditional, but it helps the seasonings stick to the dough and chars the exterior of the bread nicely. Feel free to play around with seasonings in the dough or the toppings. I like Panch Phoron (page 26) but use whatever you prefer.

Instant Pot trivet

¾ cup (175 mL) warm **water**

1 teaspoon (5 mL) active dry **yeast**

2 teaspoons (10 mL) granulated **sugar**, divided

2 cups (500 mL) **all-purpose flour** (approx.)

1 teaspoon (5 mL) **kosher salt** (approx.)

1 teaspoon (5 mL) **cumin seeds**, toasted (optional)

¼ cup (60 mL) **Plain Yogurt** (page 40) or store-bought

¼ cup (60 mL) melted **ghee**, divided (approx.)

1 cup (250 mL) boiling **water**

1 Place the warm water in a medium bowl. Sprinkle the yeast and 1 teaspoon (5 mL) sugar onto the surface of the water. Set aside for about 10 minutes, until foamy.

2 Whisk together the flour, salt, remaining 1 teaspoon (5 mL) sugar and the cumin seeds (if using) in a large bowl.

3 Add the yogurt and 2 tablespoons (30 mL) ghee to the yeast mixture; whisk until smooth. Pour into the flour mixture and fold together with a rubber spatula. Knead the dough in the bowl for about 3 minutes, until it is soft and slightly sticky.

4 Pour 1 tablespoon (15 mL) of the remaining ghee into a clean metal, ceramic or glass bowl small enough to fit inside the inner pot; add the dough and turn to coat.

5 Place the trivet inside the inner pot and add 1 cup (250 mL) boiling water. Lower the bowl of dough onto the trivet. Secure the lid and, using the Yogurt function on Normal, proof the dough for 1 hour, until it is puffy and doubled in size.

6 Transfer the dough to a floured surface and separate it into 8 equal pieces. Shape each piece into a ball, dipping your hands in flour as needed to keep the dough from sticking. Roll or stretch each piece into an oblong shape about ¼ inch (0.5 cm) thick, placing a damp dishtowel over the dough pieces so they don't dry out.

7   Heat a cast-iron or nonstick skillet on the stove over high heat for 5 minutes. Add 1 teaspoon (5 mL) ghee and heat until almost smoking. (I know, tandoor chefs cook naan without any fat. But do you have a tandoor in your house? Me neither. So let's try it this way.) Place one piece of dough in the skillet and cook for 1 minute, or until the naan is a little charred, bubbled and blistered on one side. Flip over and cook the other side for 1 minute, until the second side is lightly charred.

8   Transfer the naan to a cutting board, sprinkle kosher salt and any spices you like overtop, and cover with a dishtowel to keep warm. Repeat with the remaining pieces of dough, adding more ghee to the pan as needed.

NOTES   *This recipe doubles nicely—and who doesn't like extra bread?*

Try toasting any leftovers in the toaster. I treat leftover naan like a bagel and smear it with cream cheese for breakfast. It may not be traditional, but it's undeniably delicious.

ROTIS. VEG V

Rotis and chapatis are the same thing: a wheat flatbread served alongside curries and used to wrap up Chicken Jalfrezi Frankies (page 212). The dough is unleavened but rolls out better when it can rest for 30 minutes in a warm space, so I tuck mine into the Instant Pot and use the Yogurt function—it's the best place for dough napping.

Instant Pot trivet

2   cups (500 mL) **whole wheat flour** (approx.)
1   teaspoon (5 mL) **kosher salt**
2   teaspoons (10 mL) ground **cumin**
⅔ cup (150 mL) room-temperature **water**
¼   cup (60 mL) **vegetable oil**
1   cup (250 mL) boiling **water**

1   Combine the flour, salt and cumin in a large bowl. Make a well in the center and slowly add the room-temperature water and oil. Knead the dough in the bowl until soft and slightly sticky, adding more water if it seems too dry.

2   Place the trivet in the inner pot and add the boiling water. Place the dough in an insert pan or a clean metal, ceramic or glass bowl small enough to fit inside the inner pot. Lower the dough container onto the trivet. Secure the lid and, using the Yogurt function, let the dough rest for 30 minutes.

3   Transfer the dough to a lightly floured surface. Divide into 12 equal pieces and cover with a damp dishtowel. Working with one piece at a time, shape each piece into a ball, dipping your hands in flour as needed to keep the dough from sticking. Flatten each ball with the heel of your hand, then roll it into a 6-inch (15 cm) round.

4   Heat a cast-iron or other heavy-bottomed skillet over medium-high heat. Once it's very hot, add a dough round and cook for 1 minute, until some brown spots appear on the bottom. Flip the roti and cook for 1 minute more, until it is browned in spots. Transfer to a platter. Repeat with the remaining dough rounds, stacking them on the platter as they are cooked; serve.

NOTE *For garlic rotis, fold 2 tablespoons (30 mL) minced garlic into the dough in Step 1.*

PURIS

VEG **V** (FRIED WHOLE WHEAT FLATBREADS)

Puris, deep-fried flatbreads that are eaten all over South India, are the bread and soul of my childhood. They are both a bread and eating implement all in one, and when I was a kid, I ate them as if it were my job. I never tired of watching my mother fry them until they puffed up. When she turned her back, I'd grab one from the pile, burning my fingers on the hot bread but not caring as I folded over the chewy, crispy rounds to scoop up potatoes and chutney.

Instant Pot trivet

- 2 cups (500 mL) **all-purpose flour** (approx.)
- ¼ cup (60 mL) **whole wheat flour**
- ½ teaspoon (2 mL) **kosher salt**
- ½ cup (125 mL) warm **water**
  Vegetable oil
- 1 cup (250 mL) **water**

1 Combine the all-purpose flour, whole wheat flour and salt in a large bowl. Make a well in the center and add the warm water, mixing it into the flour.

2 Pour 1 tablespoon (15 mL) oil over the dough and knead in the bowl for 10 minutes, until soft and pliable.

3 Transfer the dough to an insert pan or a clean metal, ceramic or glass bowl small enough to fit inside the inner pot; cover with plastic wrap. Place the trivet in the inner pot and add 1 cup (250 mL) water. Place the bowl on the trivet. Secure the lid and, using the Yogurt function on Low, let the dough rise for 30 minutes.

4 Remove the dough from the inner pot and transfer to a very lightly floured surface. Shape into a long cylinder, then portion that into 12 equal pieces. Roll each piece into a ball, then flatten it into a circle about ⅛ inch (3 mm) thick.

5 Heat about 1 inch (2.5 cm) oil in a cast-iron or heavy-bottomed nonstick skillet over medium heat. Gently slide a dough round into the oil. Don't be afraid—at first it will sink, then it will rise to the top. Use a spatula to gently press down on the edges of the puri. Cook for 1 minute, until it puffs up and the bottom is brown. Using a spatula, flip over the puri and cook for 30 seconds more, until the other side has browned.

6 Using a slotted spoon, transfer the puri to a plate lined with paper towels. Repeat with the remaining dough, adding more oil to the skillet and heating between batches, as needed. Serve hot.

AMRITSARI KULCHAS

 (POTATO-STUFFED FLATBREADS)

Just when you think you can't do better than naan, you discover kulchas (stuffed breads) from Amritsar in northwestern India, and realize you have achieved bread-carb heaven. I tend to eat these with soup or as a light main course rather than alongside a curry.

DOUGH

- 2 cups (500 mL) **all-purpose flour** (approx.)
- 2 teaspoons (10 mL) granulated **sugar**
- 1 teaspoon (5 mL) **baking powder**
- 1 teaspoon (5 mL) **kosher salt**
- 1 teaspoon (5 mL) **nigella seeds**
- ½ teaspoon (2 mL) **baking soda**
- ¼ cup (60 mL) **Plain Yogurt** (page 40) or store-bought
- ½ cup (125 mL) **whole milk**, warmed
- 1 tablespoon (15 mL) **vegetable oil**

FILLING

- 1 pound (500 g) **yellow-fleshed potatoes**, chopped
- 1 cup (250 mL) **water**
- 1 teaspoon (5 mL) ground **cumin**
- 1 teaspoon (5 mL) **kosher salt**
- ½ teaspoon (2 mL) **Kashmiri chili powder**
- ½ teaspoon ((2 mL) **Chaat Masala** (page 25) or ground sumac
- ½ **red onion**, minced
- 1 **serrano chile**, minced
- ¼ cup (60 mL) minced fresh **cilantro**
  Vegetable oil

1 DOUGH Combine the flour, sugar, baking powder, salt, nigella seeds and baking soda in a large bowl. Make a well in the center.

2 Combine the yogurt and milk in a small bowl. Pour into the well in the flour mixture and mix everything together until it pulls together into a dough. Knead the dough gently in the bowl until it is soft and smooth; shape into a round. Pour oil into a medium bowl. Add the dough and turn it to coat on all sides. Cover the dough with a damp cloth and let it stand at room temperature for 1 hour.

3 FILLING Meanwhile, place the potatoes in the inner pot with the water. Secure the lid and cook on low pressure for 12 minutes (you can also cook on high pressure for 8 minutes).

4 Once the cooking is complete, quick-release the pressure. Using a slotted spoon, transfer the potatoes to a bowl, reserving the cooking water. Remove the skins, if desired, then mash the potatoes.

5 Combine the cumin, salt, chili powder and chaat masala in a small bowl. Fold the mixture into the potatoes, mixing gently but thoroughly. Fold in the onion, chile and cilantro, adding some of the reserved cooking water if the mixture is too dry and falls apart.

6 Divide the dough into 6 equal pieces. Roll each out into a flat, even disc about 6 inches (15 cm) in diameter. Let the dough rest if it contracts after it's rolled—that means it's not quite ready.

7 Scoop 3 tablespoons (45 mL) filling into the center of each round. Fold up the sides over the filling to encase it, pressing down gently to seal it in. Lightly dust each round with flour and gently roll it out into a thick, flat disc about 6 inches (15 cm) in diameter, making sure not to press out the filling.

8 Heat 3 tablespoons (45 mL) oil in a cast-iron or heavy-bottomed nonstick skillet until hot. Place 1 kulcha in the skillet and cook for 2 minutes, until golden brown; then flip it over and cook for 1 minute more, until brown on the other side. Repeat with the remaining kulchas, adding more oil to the pan as needed; serve.

• CHAPTER ELEVEN •

DESSERTS

RASMALAI CAKE

VEG **GF** (SAFFRON PANEER CAKE)

Most Indian desserts are too sweet for me, but I have always loved rasmalai. The creamy, soft paneer soaked in sweet, cardamom-spiced milk syrup gets me every time. That said, rasmalai was never something I thought I could make at home, until I tried making it as a single cake instead of several small patties, as it's usually served. This cake is a little sturdier than delicate rasmalai but retains that creamy texture. I'll eat this anytime.

7-inch (18 cm) metal baking pan with removable bottom

Instant Pot trivet

Stand mixer with whip attachment, or electric hand mixer

3 large **eggs**, separated

1½ cups (375 mL) **Soft Paneer** (page 67) or **ricotta cheese**

⅔ cup (150 mL) granulated **sugar**, divided

1 teaspoon (5 mL) **vanilla extract**

1 teaspoon (5 mL) grated **lemon zest**

¾ teaspoon (3 mL) **kosher salt**

¼ cup (60 mL) **heavy** or **whipping** (35%) **cream**

2 cups (500 mL) **water**

1 cup (250 mL) **whole milk**

10 **green cardamom pods**, crushed

Pinch **saffron**

1 teaspoon (5 mL) **rosewater**

½ cup (125 mL) finely chopped **pistachios**

¼ cup (60 mL) dried **rose petals** (optional)

1 Place the egg whites in a stand mixer bowl or large bowl. Beat, using the mixer on high speed, for about 2 minutes, until soft peaks form. Transfer the whites to a separate large bowl (if using a stand mixer).

2 Place the egg yolks, paneer, ⅓ cup (75 mL) sugar, vanilla, lemon zest, salt and cream in the mixer bowl or another large bowl. Beat, using the mixer on high speed, for about 4 minutes, until very smooth.

3 Gently fold half the egg whites into the paneer mixture, then fold in the remaining egg whites.

4 Pour the batter into the pan. Place a paper towel directly on top of the batter and cover the pan with foil. Place the trivet in the inner pot and add the water. Lower the cake onto the trivet.

5 Secure the lid and cook on high pressure for 40 minutes.

6 Let the pressure release naturally for 10 minutes, then quick-release the remaining pressure. Remove the cake from the inner pot, discarding the paper towel and foil. Let the cake cool in the pan on a rack at room temperature for 1 hour; then transfer it to the refrigerator to cool completely.

7 Meanwhile, using the Sauté function on Normal, heat the milk and cardamom pods in the inner pot until simmering. Spoon 1 tablespoon (15 mL) of the milk into a small bowl and add the saffron. Set it aside to let the saffron bloom.

8 Add the remaining ⅓ cup (75 mL) sugar to the pot and reduce the heat to Low. Simmer, stirring frequently, for about 20 minutes, until the milk has thickened slightly. Stir in the saffron-soaked milk and rosewater.

9 Remove the cake from the refrigerator and, using a toothpick or skewer, poke about a dozen holes in the top and sides. Pour the milk syrup over the cake. Let stand for at least 1 hour at room temperature or up to 8 hours refrigerated before serving. Top the cake with crushed pistachios and rose petals (if using) and serve.

NOTE *You can make the cake and the milk syrup up to 2 days in advance. Just make sure to keep them in the refrigerator in separate airtight containers. Don't soak the cake until the day you want to serve it.*

COCONUT CHOCOLATE
RAVA CAKE

 VEG (SEMOLINA CAKE)

Many kitchens in India don't have ovens, but you need something to eat with your afternoon tea, so Indians long ago figured out how to steam cakes in stovetop pressure cookers. Rava cakes, made with semolina flour, are among the most popular. The cardamom, espresso and chocolate make this cake reminiscent of a chocolate chai latte, while the coconut, chocolate and pecans in the frosting are straight out of German chocolate cake territory, with just a hint of heat from Kashmiri chili powder.

Instant Pot trivet

7-inch (18 cm) metal baking pan with removable bottom, greased

CAKE

- 1 cup (250 mL) **semolina flour**
- ¼ cup (60 mL) unsweetened **cocoa powder**
- ¾ cup (175 mL) **confectioners' (icing) sugar**
- 1 teaspoon (5 mL) ground **cardamom**
- 1 teaspoon (5 mL) instant **espresso powder**
- 1 teaspoon (5 mL) ground **cinnamon**
- ½ teaspoon (2 mL) **kosher salt**
- 1 cup (250 mL) **Plain Yogurt** (page 40) or store-bought
- ¼ cup (60 mL) melted **ghee**
- ¾ cup (175 mL) **whole milk**, divided
- 1 teaspoon (5 mL) **baking powder**
- ½ teaspoon (2 mL) **baking soda**
- 2 cups (500 mL) boiling **water**

FROSTING

- ¼ cup (60 mL) melted **ghee**
- ½ cup (125 mL) unsweetened **cocoa powder**
- 2 cups (500 mL) **confectioners' (icing) sugar**
- ½ teaspoon (2 mL) **Kashmiri chili powder**
- Pinch **kosher salt**
- ¼ cup (60 mL) **whole milk**
- 1 teaspoon (5 mL) **vanilla extract** or **bourbon**
- ½ cup (125 mL) unsweetened **coconut flakes**, toasted
- ½ cup (125 mL) **pecan pieces**, toasted (see page 32)

Recipe continues . . .

1 CAKE Whisk together the flour, cocoa powder, confectioners' sugar, cardamom, espresso powder, cinnamon and salt in a large bowl. Stir in the yogurt and ghee, then add ½ cup (125 mL) of the milk. Cover and let stand for 15 minutes, until thickened.

2 Whisk in the remaining milk, then whisk in the baking powder and baking soda. Scrape the batter into the prepared pan. Smooth out the batter, tapping the pan on the countertop to eliminate any excess bubbles.

3 Place the trivet in the inner pot and add the boiling water. Lower the cake onto the trivet. Secure the lid and, using the Steam function, steam the cake for 20 minutes, keeping the pressure valve in the Venting position. (The Instant Pot timer will not work while venting, so you'll need to set a separate timer.)

4 FROSTING Meanwhile, whisk together the ghee and cocoa powder. Then whisk in the confectioners' sugar, chili powder, salt, milk and vanilla, continuing to whisk until no lumps remain. Cover and set aside.

5 Remove the cake from the inner pot. Let cool in the pan until just warm, then remove the cake from the pan and transfer to a plate to let it cool completely.

6 Just before serving, fold the toasted coconut and pecans into the frosting. Frost the cake and serve.

NOTE *This cake comes with sound effects—keeping the vent open means that it will release steam while it cooks. (If you have cats, they will hiss back at it for your entertainment.)*

CHOCOLATE CHAI (VEG) (GF)

This pudding is decadence defined, and much more sophisticated than the pudding cups my brothers and I got as treats while visiting family in India (ahem, Mom). Here bittersweet chocolate gets a boost of flavor from a chai-infused cream, while additional chai cream on top pushes it over the edge.

6- to 7-inch (15 to 18 cm) soufflé dish or 6 ramekins (see Note)

Instant Pot trivet

Stand mixer with whip attachment, or electric hand mixer

2 cups (500 mL) **heavy** or **whipping** (35%) **cream**

3 tablespoons (45 mL) loose **chai** (from about 4 teabags)

5 ounces (150 g) bittersweet (dark) **chocolate**, chopped

3 large **egg yolks**

2 large **eggs**

⅓ cup (75 mL) **jaggery** or **brown sugar**

1 teaspoon (5 mL) **vanilla extract**

½ teaspoon (2 mL) **kosher salt**

1 cup (250 mL) boiling **water**

1 tablespoon (15 mL) granulated **sugar**

NOTE *You can make 6 individual puddings instead of one large pudding; simply divide the mixture among six ½-cup (125 mL) ramekins or oven-safe cups. Place 3 on the trivet and cover with a piece of foil; then carefully stack the other 3 ramekins on top and cover them with a piece of foil. Secure the lid and cook the puddings on high pressure for 4 minutes.*

1 Combine the cream and loose chai in a medium saucepan over medium-low heat; bring to a simmer. Turn off the heat and let stand for 30 minutes.

2 Return the cream to a simmer, then strain through a fine-mesh sieve into a medium bowl. Reserve ½ cup (125 mL) cream, cover and refrigerate. Pour the remaining cream over the chocolate in another medium bowl; whisk until the chocolate is melted and the mixture is smooth.

3 Whisk together the egg yolks, eggs, jaggery, vanilla and salt in a large bowl. Gradually add the chocolate mixture, whisking constantly for about 1 minute, until smooth.

4 Pour the pudding into the soufflé dish and wrap the dish with foil. Place the trivet in the inner pot and add the boiling water. Lower the dish onto the trivet. Secure the lid and cook on high pressure for 8 minutes.

5 Once the cooking is complete, release the pressure naturally for 5 minutes, then quick-release the remaining pressure. Remove the dish from the inner pot and discard the foil. Let the pudding cool to room temperature. Chill in the refrigerator for at least 3 hours or up to 2 days.

6 Just before serving, place the reserved cream and sugar in a stand mixer bowl or large bowl. Beat on high speed for 1 to 2 minutes, until soft peaks form.

7 Divide the pudding between 6 small bowls. Add a dollop of whipped cream to each; serve.

PREP
10 MIN

MANUAL
12 MIN

RELEASE
NATURAL/ QUICK

TOTAL
40 MIN

SERVES
6

CARROT HALWA CAKE

If you go to a festival or holiday dinner in India, you'll likely eat carrot halwa, which is a dense, thick pudding made from grated carrots simmered in ghee and cream. This dessert is what happens when that halwa has a baby with a classic American carrot cake and combines complex spices with the tangy cream cheese frosting. It's the best of both worlds.

Stand mixer with whip attachment, or electric hand mixer

7-inch (18 cm) metal baking pan with removable bottom, greased

Instant Pot trivet

CAKE

- 1 cup (250 mL) **all-purpose flour**
- 2 teaspoons (10 mL) ground **cardamom**
- 1 teaspoon (5 mL) **kosher salt**
- 1 teaspoon (5 mL) ground **cinnamon**
- 1 teaspoon (5 mL) **baking powder**
- ½ teaspoon (2 mL) ground **nutmeg**
- 2½ cups (625 mL) grated **carrots**
- 1 cup (250 mL) chopped raw **cashews**, toasted (see page 32)
- ¾ cup (175 mL) **jaggery powder** or **brown sugar**
- ½ cup (125 mL) melted **ghee** or **melted butter**
- 2 large **eggs**
- 1 teaspoon (5 mL) **vanilla extract** or **bourbon**
- 1 cup (250 mL) boiling **water**

FROSTING

- 8 ounces (250 g) brick-style **cream cheese**, softened
- ¼ cup (60 mL) **Plain Yogurt** (page 40) or store-bought
- ¼ cup (60 mL) **confectioners' (icing) sugar**
- 1 teaspoon (5 mL) **vanilla extract** or **bourbon**
- ½ teaspoon (2 mL) ground **cardamom**
- ¼ cup (60 mL) chopped **pistachios**

1 **CAKE** Whisk together the flour, cardamom, salt, cinnamon, baking powder and nutmeg in a large bowl. Fold in the carrots and cashews.

2 Combine the jaggery, ghee, eggs and vanilla in a stand mixer bowl or large bowl. Beat, using the mixer on high speed, for about 2 minutes, until smooth.

3 Add the jaggery mixture to the flour mixture and fold until just combined. Scrape the batter into the prepared pan and place a paper towel directly on top of the batter.

4 Place the trivet in the inner pot and add the boiling water. Lower the cake onto the trivet. Secure the lid and cook on high pressure for 12 minutes.

5 **FROSTING** Meanwhile, whisk together the cream cheese, yogurt, confectioners' sugar, vanilla and cardamom until smooth. Cover the frosting until ready to use.

6 Let the pressure release naturally for 10 minutes, then quick-release the remaining pressure.

7 Remove the cake from the inner pot and let it cool in the pan until just warm. Remove the cake from the pan, discarding the paper towel. Transfer to a wire rack and let cool completely. Slice the cake into 6 pieces. Smear a large dollop of frosting onto each of 6 plates, then top it with a piece of cake. Garnish with pistachios and serve.

ORANGE CARDAMOM VEG
CHEESECAKE

Cheesecake happens to be one of the best things you can make in an Instant Pot, since the best cheesecakes are cooked in a water bath anyway. Although traditional New York–style cheesecakes can be quite dense, this one is light and creamy, with citrusy, spicy flavors.

7-inch (18 cm) metal baking pan with removable bottom

Stand mixer with whip attachment, or electric hand mixer

Instant Pot trivet

CRUST

- 2 cups (500 mL) **graham cracker** or **spice cookie crumbs**
- ½ cup (125 mL) granulated **sugar**, divided
- 1 teaspoon (5 mL) **kosher salt**, divided
- 6 tablespoons (90 mL) **ghee** or **melted butter**

FILLING

- 1 pound (500 g) brick-style **cream cheese**, softened
- 2 teaspoons (10 mL) **orange extract**
- 2 teaspoons (10 mL) freshly squeezed **orange juice**
- 2 large **eggs**, at room temperature
- 1 teaspoon (5 mL) ground **cardamom**
- 2 tablespoons (30 mL) grated **orange zest**
- 1½ cups (375 mL) **water**

1 CRUST Preheat the oven to 350°F (180°C).

2 Combine the graham cracker crumbs, ¼ cup (60 mL) sugar and a pinch of salt in a large bowl. Pour in the ghee and mix until the crumbs are evenly coated.

Using the bottom of a glass, press the crumbs into an even layer on the bottom and up the sides of the baking pan. Bake in the preheated oven for 15 minutes, until the crust is fragrant and set. Transfer to a wire rack for about 30 minutes to cool completely.

3 FILLING Combine the cream cheese and the remaining ¼ cup (60 mL) sugar in a stand mixer bowl or large bowl. Beat, using the mixer on medium-high speed, for about 2 minutes, until the batter is very smooth and no lumps remain, scraping down the sides of the bowl as needed. Beat in the orange extract, orange juice and remaining salt. Add the eggs one at a time, beating on low speed until just combined (don't overbeat the eggs or the top of the cheesecake will crack when it cooks). Stir in the cardamom.

4 Pour the filling into the crust, smoothing the top; then sprinkle it with the orange zest.

5 Wrap the pan with foil. Place the trivet in the inner pot and add the water. Lower the cake onto the trivet. Secure the lid and cook on high pressure for 35 minutes.

6 Once the cooking is complete, let the pressure release naturally for 10 minutes, then quick-release the remaining pressure. Remove the cheesecake from the inner pot and remove and discard the foil. Chill the cake in the refrigerator for at least 4 hours or up to 2 days before serving.

7 To remove the cheesecake from the pan, run a knife around the sides of the pan, then remove the sides. Transfer the cake to a platter and serve.

NOTE *If you don't have a baking pan with a removable bottom, you can use a traditional stovetop pressure cooker insert pan for this recipe. Fold a 12-inch (30 cm) piece of aluminum foil in thirds. Line the pan with the folded foil, leaving the edges hanging over the sides, before pressing in the crust. Make sure to chill the cooked cheesecake completely; then use the foil sling to pull it out of the pan.*

SPICED PUMPKIN CHEESECAKE VEG

So many Indian spices, like garam masala, coriander and cloves, work really well with pumpkin, making this cheesecake almost inevitable. It's kind of perfect if you want to make something a little different for Thanksgiving without setting off the traditionalists at your table. The cheesecake is pretty fantastic on its own, but the Garam Masala Salt Caramel Sauce (page 277) takes it to extreme dessert heaven.

Food processor

7-inch (18 cm) baking pan with removable bottom

Stand mixer with whip attachment, or electric hand mixer

Instant Pot trivet

CRUST

- 2 cups (500 mL) **gingersnap** or **graham cracker crumbs**
- ¼ cup (60 mL) granulated **sugar**
  Pinch **kosher salt**
- 6 tablespoons (90 mL) melted **ghee** or **melted butter**

FILLING

- 1 pound (500 g) brick-style **cream cheese**, softened
- 1 cup (250 mL) canned **pumpkin purée** (not pie filling)
- ½ cup (125 mL) granulated **sugar**
- 1 teaspoon (5 mL) **vanilla extract**
- 1 teaspoon (5 mL) ground **cinnamon**
- ½ teaspoon (2 mL) ground **ginger**
- ½ teaspoon (2 mL) **Garam Masala** (page 24) or store-bought
- 1 teaspoon (5 mL) **kosher salt**
- ¼ teaspoon (1 mL) ground **nutmeg**
- ¼ teaspoon (1 mL) ground **cloves**
- 2 large **eggs**, at room temperature
- 1½ cups (375 mL) **water**

1 **CRUST** Preheat the oven to 350°F (180°C).

2 Pulse the gingersnap crumbs, sugar and salt in a food processor until finely ground. Add the ghee and pulse a few times to combine.

3 Using the bottom of a glass, press the crumbs into an even layer on the bottom and up the sides of the baking pan. Bake the crust in the preheated oven for 15 minutes, until fragrant and set. Transfer to a wire rack to cool completely.

4 **FILLING** Combine the cream cheese, pumpkin, sugar, vanilla, cinnamon, ginger, garam masala, salt, nutmeg and cloves in a stand mixer bowl or large bowl. Beat, using the mixer on high speed, for about 2 minutes, until light and creamy, scraping down the sides of the bowl as needed. Add the eggs one at a time, beating on low speed until just combined (don't overbeat the eggs or the top of the cheesecake will crack when it cooks). Pour the batter into the crust and smooth the top.

5 Wrap the pan with foil. Place the trivet in the inner pot and add the water. Lower the cheesecake onto the trivet. Secure the lid and cook on high pressure for 43 minutes.

6 Once the cooking is complete, let the pressure release naturally for 10 minutes, then quick-release the remaining pressure. Remove the cheesecake from the inner pot. Remove and discard the foil. Chill the cheesecake in the refrigerator for at least 4 hours or up to 2 days.

7 To remove the cheesecake from the pan, run a knife around the sides of the pan, then remove the sides. If there is condensation on top of the cheesecake, blot it gently with a paper towel. Transfer the cake to a platter and serve.

SAFFRON KHEER

WITH CARDAMOM POACHED PEARS

  (RICE PUDDING)

My wonderful mother-in-law is the kind of person who stops by to drop off something she knows you will love, then races off to her next community meeting or event. When she gave me a dozen pears from a friend's tree, I pounced on them, knowing that cardamom-poached pears were in my future. A quick bath in white wine and honey softens the pears and makes them ideal partners for the floral notes from the rice cooked in saffron-flecked cream.

8 **green cardamom pods**, cracked

1 cup (250 mL) dry **white wine** (see Notes, on opposite page)

1 cup (250 mL) **water** (approx.)

½ cup (125 mL) **honey**

2 tablespoons (30 mL) freshly squeezed **lemon juice**

1 tablespoon (15 mL) **kosher salt**, divided (approx.)

4 ripe but firm **Bosc** or **Anjou pears**, peeled and cut into large wedges

1 tablespoon (15 mL) **ghee**

¾ cup (175 mL) **white rice**

3 cups (750 mL) **whole milk**

¼ cup (60 mL) granulated **sugar** (approx.)

Pinch **saffron**

½ cup (125 mL) **heavy** or **whipping** (35%) **cream** (approx.)

¼ cup (60 mL) chopped **hazelnuts**, toasted (page 32)

1 Place the cardamom pods, wine, water, honey, lemon juice and 1½ teaspoons (7 mL) salt in the inner pot. Using the Sauté function on High, bring the mixture to a simmer, stirring occasionally, for about 5 minutes, until the honey dissolves.

2 Add the pears to the inner pot, making sure they are submerged completely in the poaching liquid; add more water as needed.

3 Secure the lid and cook on high pressure for 4 minutes.

4 Once the cooking is complete, quick-release the pressure.

5 Using a slotted spoon, remove the pears and transfer to a medium bowl. Using the Sauté function on Normal, simmer the poaching liquid for about 10 to 15 minutes, until it reduces down to 1 cup (250 mL). Transfer to a container and let it stand at room temperature until ready to use. Clean the inner pot.

6 Using the Sauté function on High, heat the ghee in the inner pot for about 1 minute, until shimmering. Add the rice and stir for 30 seconds, until coated in ghee. Stir in the remaining 1½ teaspoons (7 mL) salt, milk, sugar and saffron. Secure the lid and cook, using the Porridge function (it will automatically set the cooking time to 20 minutes).

7 Once the cooking is complete, let the pressure release naturally.

8 Remove the lid and mash about half of the rice with the back of a spoon or ladle. Using the Sauté function on Low, simmer, stirring constantly to keep the rice from sticking to the bottom of the pot, until thick and creamy. Stir in about half of the cream; add more as needed to adjust the consistency to your preference. Taste and add more sugar or salt as needed. The kheer can be kept on Warm mode for up to 1 hour until you are ready to serve, or transfer to the refrigerator to chill for up to 2 days. (Keep in mind that the kheer will thicken as it cools, so if you're planning to keep it warm or refrigerate it, thin it out with a little more water.)

9 Divide the kheer between 4 bowls and top each with pears and syrup. Garnish with toasted hazelnuts; serve.

NOTES *You can poach the pears up to a day in advance of serving them. Complete the recipe to the end of Step 5 and store them in an airtight container in the refrigerator. Bring to room temperature before serving.*

If you don't want to use wine in the poaching liquid, simply substitute an additional 1 cup (250 mL) water mixed with 1 tablespoon (15 mL) freshly squeezed lemon juice.

LIME COCONUT
KHEER
WITH TOASTED PISTACHIOS

   (SWEET AND TANGY RICE PUDDING)

Kheer is often served on festival days. It has a reputation for being heavy, but I think the lime and coconut milk in this recipe make it light, even tropical. You can serve this pudding hot, at room temperature or chilled (it's a pretty fantastic midnight snack straight out of the fridge). As a bonus, this super-creamy dessert is vegan.

1 cup (250 mL) **white rice**, rinsed (see Note)

1 can (14 oz/398 mL) full-fat **coconut milk**

1 cup (250 mL) **water** (approx.)

¾ cup (175 mL) granulated **sugar**

1 tablespoon (15 mL) minced **ginger**

1 teaspoon (5 mL) **kosher salt**

1 cup (250 mL) unsweetened **coconut flakes**

3 tablespoons (45 mL) grated **lime zest**, divided

1 tablespoon (15 mL) freshly squeezed **lime juice**

¾ cup (175 mL) chopped **pistachios**

1 Place the rice, coconut milk, water, sugar, ginger, salt and coconut in the inner pot; stir to combine. Secure the lid and select the Porridge function (it will automatically set the cooking time to 20 minutes).

2 Once the cooking is complete, let the pressure release naturally for 5 minutes, then quick-release the remaining pressure.

3 Mash about half of the rice with the back of a spoon or ladle. Stir in 2 tablespoons (30 mL) lime zest and the lime juice. (The pudding should be thick and creamy. If not, using the Sauté function on Low, simmer it, stirring constantly to keep the rice from sticking to the bottom of the pot, until it reaches your preferred consistency.) The kheer can be kept on Warm mode for up to 1 hour until you are ready to serve, or transfer it to the refrigerator to chill for up to 2 days. (Keep in mind that the kheer will thicken as it cools, so if you're planning to keep it warm or refrigerate it, thin it out with a little more water.) Spoon into 6 bowls and top with the remaining 1 tablespoon (15 mL) lime zest and pistachios; serve.

NOTE *You can also make the kheer with 3 cups (750 mL) leftover cooked rice. Just use half the amount of coconut milk and cook it for 10 minutes on low pressure.*

PREP
5 MIN

SAUTÉ
8 MIN

TOTAL
15 MIN

MAKES
1½ CUPS
(375 ML)

GARAM MASALA SALTED CARAMEL SAUCE

VEG • GF

I can be counted on to have a tub of this caramel sauce in my refrigerator at all times. It comes in handy when I need to figure out a dessert on the fly (caramel sauce + ice cream and/or cookies = YES) or want a little something extra to serve with a cheesecake or brownies—or the equally important mid-afternoon emergency spoonful straight from the fridge. Making caramel sauce is very easy. Just be sure you respect the sauce, and don't touch it while it's cooking or right afterward, even if its sweet goodness beckons you to try it. Sugar holds a lot of heat, and you don't want to burn yourself.

1   cup (250 mL) granulated **sugar**

¼   cup (60 mL) **water**

½   cup (125 mL) **heavy** or **whipping** (35%) **cream**, warmed (approx.)

2   tablespoons (30 mL) unsalted **butter**

1   teaspoon (5 mL) **kosher salt**

1   Place the sugar and water in the inner pot and stir together. Using the Sauté function on Normal, heat the mixture for about 8 minutes, until the sugar dissolves and turns light brown. Tilt the Instant Pot occasionally to move around the caramelizing sugar, but do not stir it (stirring will make the caramel crystallize).

2   Turn off the heat and let the sauce rest for 3 minutes. (The residual heat will cause it to darken a bit.).

3   Stir in the cream a little at a time; the caramel will bubble with each addition, so you don't want to add all the cream at once. Stir in the butter and salt until melted and smooth. Stir in more cream if the sauce is too thick for your taste. Serve immediately or store in an airtight container in the refrigerator for up to 10 days (and you are a hero if it lasts that long). Heat it before serving, if you prefer.

ACKNOWLEDGMENTS

This book would still be a document glaring
at me from my laptop were it not for a lot of people whose
hard work made it a reality.

Thank you to my fabulous agent AMY COLLINS, who raved about the Instant Pot so much that I had to get one, and then convinced me to write this book in the time it took us to drive home from dinner. Thank you for your ideas, encouragement, patience and grace through all the midnight texts and phone calls. I'm lucky to have you as an agent and a friend.

Thank you to my dear editor MEREDITH DEES, for seeing this book's potential, thoughtfully editing it, patiently reworking the schedule, and cheering me on in endless editorial comments, emails and texts. And many thanks to the rest of the TEAM AT ROBERT ROSE, especially Bob Dees (for ALL your support), Kelly Glover, Jennifer MacKenzie, Nina McCreath, Martine Quibell and Gillian Watts.

To LAURA PALESE, your design gives this book all the life and energy of India; thank you.

To HUGE GALDONES: You, sir, are my Motownphilly. I can't thank you enough for sharing your creative talent, time, energy, generous spirit and carnitas with me and this book. I am so grateful I got to work with you.

To CHRISTINA ZERKIS: I don't know what would have happened without you guiding me through the photo shoot, but know it wouldn't have been pretty. Thank you for your ideas and talent, and for saving this book from my crappy cilantro garnishes.

Thank you to the rest of the PHOTO SHOOT SQUAD: Tom Van Lente, Ben Macri, Lorenzo Tassone, Shannon Kinsella, Stacey Ballis, Lili McGovern, Gabrielle Sukich, and Todd Schnack. I would be weeping over a pot of biryani were it not for your hard work and good spirits throughout the shoot. And thanks to the crew at SKALAWAG PRODUCTIONS for all the smiles and "smells good in here!" when we were surely driving you crazy.

To the RECIPE TESTING CREW, who were kind with advice even when dinner didn't work out. Thank you for helping make sure these recipes really work: Josh Ackerman, Tatiana Alexandrovna, Helen Baldus, Ari Bendersky, Barbara Bohn, CeCe Campise, Amy Cavanaugh, Jennifer Chan, Julie Chernoff, Panchi Cole, Margaret Eby, Lisa Futterman, Cameron Grant, Liz Grossman, Drew Harris, Shebnem Ince, Gabby Juocys, Shannon Kinsella, Kat Kinsman, Tony McClung, Lizzy Magarian, Elana Margolis, Jen Mayer, Laura Oldham, Amy Orlando, Emily Paster, Rajeev Patgaonkar, Connie Pikulas, Kathryn Renna, Lisa Shames, Mike Sula, Erika Wilder, Paige Worthy and Claudia Anthony Zompa.

To my dear cousin NEERU BOMMAKANTI: Thank you for your guidance, friendship, encouragement and all those hours of talking me though idli batter. Thank you UNCLE MADHAV and AUNTIE SAROJANI for all your advice and encouragement. And thank you to SURYA, TEJAS, KAVI and MANAS for the Indian history lessons, encouragement and queso breaks.

To my FAMILY AND FRIENDS: Thank you for cheering me on, and for your patience through all the cooking mishaps forced upon you at dinner parties and understanding for all the unreturned phone calls and texts.

To my MOTHER, who fearlessly jumped into Indian cooking decades ago and taught me how to cook as she modeled how to be an incredible human being. I am so lucky to be your daughter.

To my husband, JAY. I couldn't have done this book without your love, support and endless appetite for leftovers. Thank you for making my dreams come true.

INDEX